THE SEVENTIES:

Counterfeit Decade

Herbert London

University Press
of America™

THE SEVENTIES: COUNTERFEIT DECADE

Preface

Introduction: An Essay on the Seventies

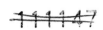

III. Education

PREFACE

Recently I asked a student to compare the sixties and the seventies. "How do you remember these decades?" I inquired. "The seventies is dullsville," was the response. "Dullsville?", I asked. "Yeah, a period where nothing is going on."

This student was probably right. In many ways this decade is dullsville. But why is this true?

Throughout this decade I tried to answer the question by addressing myself to cultural, social and political change. Hopefully these articles reveal something of the national mood. This book is neither sociology, nor history in any strict sense. It is one man's comment about this period, an inquiry into its origin and meaning.

I recognize my own cultural legacy and hence my limitations. I am more a product of the fifties than the sixties and, as a consequence, feel more comfortable now than ten years ago. But what I've tried to do is make sense of my feelings in the chapters that follow. If the reader is somewhat close to an understanding of this decade through a reading of these pages, then my goal will have been achieved. If the reader - at least - understands my sentiments, then my sense of communication will be satisfied. And if this book does nothing

but make some people bilious, then my instinct for
controversy will be confirmed.

Herbert Ira London

Introduction

The seventies arrived as an anticlimax. After
a period of social upheaval, that could be expected.
Even Watergate was, in many respects, a response to
conditions and attitudes fomented in the sixties. In
a symbolic way it marked the end of one era and the
beginning of another.

But what of this decade? Did it, like every
other period of the century, have its own idiosyncratic
style? Was it - as many social analysts allege -
the fifties all over again? Could it be viewed in
marked contrast with the sixties, a period at odds
with the prevailing sentiments of the immediate past?

In most ways the seventies is a paradox. Without question in tenor and style it is different from
the sixties. But the cultural legacy of the preceding
decade is not entirely rejected. The seventies might
be described as a Thermidorean reaction. A cultural
revolution that promoted abstract ideals could not
possibly obtain public support. But, liberated from
what was believed to be the provincialism of
bourgeois virtue, the clock could not be turned back.
Cultural leaders recognizing the national mood have
tried to retain the spirit of the revolution and,
simultaneously, to offer assurances that violent
swings in behavior would not occur again - at least

not soon again.

The seventies has been a time of repose, a chance to collect one's thoughts. It is not "back to normalcy" nor is it a "new frontier." It is a moment for the culture to catch its breath. Perhaps that explains why there has been so little unique cultural activity. Since the nation is seeking repose, the culture has turned to those moments in the past when meaning was clear, virtue upheld. Popular programming has recalled the fifties. "Grease" and "Happy Days" are recollections of a time when social values - however vacuous - were well understood. Mom and Dad stood by their children. The corner drugstore was a safe refuge from the battering of peer group pressures. And support for one's friends was an unspoken obligation. The sixties may have undermined those values. But in this decade there are questions raised about the cost-benefits of social destruction. A cultural synthesis is sought, even if it cannot yet be achieved.

This decade is an interregnum - a time between distinctive eras. The population gropes for meaning in its lives; but essentially the groping is an attempt to reestablish norms that are shared and well understood. I have described the seventies as the counterfeit decade because it has no unique character

CHAPTER 1
WHAT'S IN IT FOR 'POOR LITTLE ME'?

Now that the Bicentennial bravura has come and gone, a somewhat dispassionate analysis of this nation is once again possible.

The paeans to our past glory and the apocalyptic visions of the future are part of this celebration, but only part. As a nation America is not what it was and far from what it can be.

If the Bicentennial marks a period of decline, as is so often alleged, it is due less to environmental problems, foreign adventures, balance of trade problems, inflation and almost any of the causes that frequntly appear in the newspapers.

It seems to me the American malaise, to the extent it is discernible, can be attributed most appropriately to the "Poor Little Me" factor, that ubiquitous aspect of contemporary life characterized by a combination of despair and self-indulgence.

Americans have become so preoccupied with the often described hopelessness of the technological age that they ignore whatever rays of hope exist.

We hear about assassinations, crime, nuclear incineration, biological tampering and rarely a word about polio's elimination, our standard of living, the national parks and our relative freedom.

We have so extended our egos that a new language

of self-indulgence has emerged. We are not lonely, but alienated. We are not sad, but down. Pretension abounds. Our heroes have been expunged from the past. The self as hero has unfolded as the principle of an age in which vanity is everything and nothing but the self is quite good enough.

THE POOR LITTLE MES are up against it. "Times are tough", or "I just can't cope," or "Why does it always happen to me?" are the continual laments. These are the Charlie Browns asking "Why is everybody always pickin' on me?"

The future is bleak, the money never quite enough and the marriage unfulfilled. The Rolling Stones are contemporary Furies singing "I can't get no satis- faction." Yet satisfaction, as every philosopher from Plato to Feiffer knows, is a perceptual question. And we don't have it because what we have is not enough. It is not only that "more is worse " - as Kingsley Amis contended - but that anything we don't have makes our lives worse.

This phenomenon is what I refer to as the Ptole- maic theory of psychology. It translates into the axiom that if the planets don't revolve around me something is wrong. We are a nation of 200 million- plus suns in search of a galaxy.

2

The human potential movement has provided all
of the necessary pseudo-scientific jargon for self-
indulgence, except now it's called actualizing or,
as my mother's friends say about their children,
"finding one's self."

And where does this leave us? Searching for
illusions to nurture the self, we have been trapped
by advertising approaches that make us big, smile
brightly, move quickly and smell sweetly. But after
we've eaten, brushed, accelerated and sprayed we're
not so different after all.

There was a time 50 years ago or less when the
future held out optimism. It wasn't a particularly
disingenuous era nor was it particularly sophisticated.
But those times give life meaning because there was
a belief that our efforts would bear fruit. From
a pick and ax a nation was born.

The self could be subordinated to the national
purpose - not eliminated, mind you but kept in check
by working together for commonly held goals.

As our purpose became less clear, our vanities
were less burdened. "Poor Little Me" rose to new
heights like an unfastened balloon. A nation that
quite rightly eschews tyranny and has lost sight
of its direction, is left with little more than self-

indulgence.

The "Poor Little Me" factor is our national
creed. It is lamentably the one universal fact in
this ever more pluralistic land. "This land is your
land, this land is my land," especially my land.

Our citizens scream for more, yet when they
get more enjoy it less. We are poor only in the
sense that we are impoverished for values; for values
that give us direction and our lives meaning.

"Poor Little Me" has entered the national consciousness as Screwtape would have relished: the
more it concerns us the more it puts us in the grip
of despair and disillusion.

CHAPTER 2

THE DISAPPEARANCE OF CULTURAL VITALITY

For most of American history, culture - both mass and high - has depended on a newly arrived sense of consciousness for its vitality. The emergence of jazz, for example, suggested as much about Southern black feelings as it did about musical evolution. Episodic events such as World War II were analyzed by cultural pathologists who sought fresh perspectives from which to envision an altered relationship between the individual and society. New ways of feeling and being were the generational terrain to be conquered by cultural explorers seeking the uncharted and unknown. Even when experiences and sometimes a perspective were shared by a substantial part of the cohort group, it took the idiosyncratic imagination of the artist to make it understandable.

There was a time when an immanent subculture became a fertile ground for testing cultural assumptions because - precisely because - it was different or novel. The subcultural experience brought a dimension to the larger culture that gave it new meaning. That time no longer exists. Contemporary culture has destroyed the need for novelty. The process of cultural homogenization has now been abetted by the ubiquitous rerun. Our culture has become self-inflicted with parasitism. Our artists produce more

of what we have already experienced. And our reality
is an oblique vision of the past constructed from
the detritus of popular programs. By looking at
culture through a mirror, the artist has surrendered
the present to the past. But this is not a past
that informs; history seemingly exists not for itself,
but in order to produce the present. This arrogant
interpretation reduces all past events into the Pro-
crustean bed of contemporary media presentations.

The pragmatic distillation of history has created
the dawn-age conviction that we were all born yesterday. And in a rather curious way this has become
true. Nostalgia so dominates culture that what was,
now is and what is ,is only vaguely associated with
what was. The memory is befogged by the cultural
confusion. A media hype declares that the De Laurentiis
version of KING KONG is the "most exciting, original
motion picture event of all time..." Was there an
earlier version or was Fay Wray a fantasy of my atavistic desire?

It is not that the medium is the message, but
that the message is the familiar. Contemporary culture
thrives on deja vu. A whole generation now obtains
cultural nourishment from recycled kitsch. Superman
is the subject of a new film. Little Orphan Annie

inspired a new musical. And a character with a d.a. and a black leather jacket who keeps saying "cool it" like a broken "45" from the fifties is the reigning king of television ratings.

The distinctive symbols of this era cannot be found. Reproductive and derivational culture is what the seventies are all about. We look backwards not out of choice, but because we don't have the imagination to create a unique present. When those cultural stars do appear in our galaxy of electronic waste they are quickly consumed. Talent is not revealed but manufactured. And as is the case with all of our manufactured products ,they are eaten and disposed of without so much as a reading of the contents.

It was Daniel Boorstin among others who described America as a land that was "becoming", a vision of an incomplete and developing future. Foreigners, who were inclined to write about such things, were impressed by America's commitment to novelty which translated into a messianic devotion to change. New York, for example, was not seen as one city but as a series of cities in constant repair, face-lifting and construction by each generation that found itself in the five boroughs. Monuments were made to the

present because of a self-conscious resistance to
the tyranny of precedent. The driving cultural
force was improvement and its instrumentality, change.
That change was sometimes mindless is undeniable.
That culture often treated history with insouciance
is equally obvious. But on balance this seemed
like a small price to pay in order to sustain the
myth of an optimistic future.

"More of the same," it might be argued by Americans, was for Europeans who had trapped themselves
in an entangling love affair with the past. In this
land, on the other hand, there was a religious acceptance of more, what's "better" and the unique. Our
faith was in the indeterminate future that William
James made an American creed. It was unAmerican
to be Marxist because Marx had foreclosed on our
future and in so doing committed the unpardonable
heresy.

But what subversive politics could not accomplish,
culture has. Media programming is as predictable
as the Marxist dialectic. In their insidious way,
the media have created the illusion that all life
is interchangeable, that unique subcultural values
are unimportant. The belief that individual will
can determine the future has succumbed to the reality

4

of television reruns. Individual will seems to end where channel selection begins. In a rather ironic way the fruits of capitalist activity have achieved a goal only the most doctrinaire Marxists really thought could be realized.

Since the dawning of the television age reality has become elusive. The documentary fades in and out of our memory as news and drama. What is genuine cannot be discerned in the montage of media-staged events. Tele-drama (those events fabricated for viewers) confused matters even more by fostering the illusion that "you are there" when in fact all that you see are authentic appurtenances for an inauthentic event. Cynicism is a peer group expectation borne of incredulity. The war in Vietnam seems like the latest manifestation of media manipulation. The Olympics are not athletic competition but television-staged heroics. Demonstrations are not the ventilation of anger but media parades to satisfy the viewers.

For a generation that has been educated by television programmers, relativism can be the only learned response. There is no real and unreal, no genuine and false. There is only what is. In this era where so much of what we see is false, seeing

5

is not believing. Our judgments are often confused
by what we see. The past comes to us restored as
the present and filtered through the values of pseudo-
events. The Korean War is the setting for a situation
comedy (MASH), the Cuban missile crisis in a tele-
drama and President Kennedy's assassination a tele-
trial.

With this kind of historical restoration as
media kitsch, the future is behind us. What we
will have are reruns of what we've already seen.
It is predictable because contemporary culture follows
technique. STAR WARS is warmed-over Buck Rogers
with a dash of STAR TREK. However, as the "media
event of the decade" (see TIME magazine) it will
spawn several imitations. Because of the commercial
success of this film, any science fiction movie
must duplicate the visual techniques in STAR WARS
or risk its credibility. The dated theme of inter-
planetary strife has been restyled in the fashion
of modern technique and for the foreseeable future
will dictate the development of one phase of our
culture.

The distinctive in the culture has been so deval-
ued by repetition that "stylists" are those who
popularize a year from our recent past. WOMEN'S

WEAR DAILY reports that the next big fashion trend
will be the mini-skirt trend of 1966. Pierre Cardin
designers recently discovered the 1943 look of army
fatigues. And Anne Klein seems intent on having
us remember the depression of 1937 - only the clothes,
of course, since her prices bear no resemblance
to those of depression years.

Popular music gives us more of what was except
that now a background of Latin rhythm is employed
for everything from Beethoven's FIFTH to AIN'T SHE
SWEET. Originality becomes a hindrance to musical
interpretation that relies on the formula of disco-
sound. In fact, the song can be anything since
the style is what counts.

For cultural elitists who maintain that this
was always the case in the popular arts, it should
be pointed out that James Bond, vintage Hitchcock
films, Captain Marvel and Elvis Presley were manufactured from the imagination of entrepreneurs as
eager to expand their bank accounts as their contemporary counterparts. Yet they managed to produce
cultural figures that were entertaining, occasionally
edifying, and often original, while seventies examples of mass cult are simply stupefying.

Even the novelist of the seventies has one monotonous, self-indulgent message: fulfillment. But his idealistic goal invariable surrenders to the emotional fact of narcissistic preoccupation. Like the disco rhythm that inevitably converts all music into one sound, the contemporary novelist reduces all themes to self-appreciation. When all relationships fail, when the support of traditional institutions is unavailable, all that remains is the self-providing pleasures for its limitless delectation.

With such serious artistic work demonstrating an obsession with technique and with the popular arts exclusively imitative, culture cannot easily navigate the straits between Scylla and Charybdis. The effect of this cultural battering is not benign. What has emerged is an apocalyptic view of society that suggest decline. The future, which was once filled with opportunity, is now characterized as riddled with insoluble problems. This - it seems to me - is a cultural legacy. The vitality needed to restore a positive vision of the future, is the same vitality so sorely lacking in the arts. Perhaps space travel will restore our positive future; perhaps the limits of technique will generate a renaissance in the arts. But for the time being it is not exaggerated to describe the seventies as the decade when cultural vitality disappeared.

CHAPTER 3

CASUALTY IN AN URBAN WAR

They came to the cities in droves, those children
of the '60s who wore idealism as their armor and
pumped themselves up with the messianism of their
times. They sought out the poor, blacks and Hispanics
the way Marcus Welby gravitates to the infirm.

They desperately wanted to help. In search
of their salvation they served broth to Bowery bums,
painted psychedelic colors on decaying buildings
and sometimes brought momentary smiles to the down-
trodden. It has often been said that they were
naive, self-serving, dogmatic and Janus-faced, but
it is also true that many were in the vanguard of
neighborhood improvements and some even were casual-
ties in what is most accurately described as an
urban war. This is a story about one of these casual-
ties.

A young woman of 17 came to New York from a
sleepy suburb of Utica. She wore her uniform of
bluejean overalls and torn sneakers and she was
eager to begin a liberal arts program at New York
University. More than the university education,
it was the city that really turned her on. From
the time she was in junior high she had been primed
to work for social justice. And where better to
realize that goal than the inner city, which attracts

social deviates like fly paper?

It is only a one hour flight from Utica to New York, but the distance is actually a million miles. Susan knew that she would be making that trip one day. In her social group at home she was the astronaut of social commitment eager to seek a moon called "the just society."

"She was always sure of what she wanted," her mother said. She pursued her mission the way evangelicals pursue their entry into heaven. The question isn't whether one will get there but when.

Her parents are warm and loving people. They provided her with encouragement, protection and all of the privileges that are normally conferred on an upper-middle class kid. But the rite of passage through adolescence was painful. For Susan's mind was also made up; she had a glib answer for most questions and few questions for most comments. What could her parents do? "She had a mind of her own," they said. That remark was usually made at the moments of greatest frustration.

Susan never found her university work taxing. And she was preoccupied with her social life. Finding a mate who was as socially conscious as she happened to be wasn't easy. At least that's what she said. Her hard luck in finding a boyfriend may have been because Susan wasn't much to look at. The overalls she always wore hid her figure, so there was no way of knowing how attractive she actually was. But she finally found a prince charming who wore baggy overalls and championed the "real people" and lived on the Lower East Side. It wasn't what the middle class would call "a relationship made in heaven."

They constantly tested each other's commitment to radicalism. Late into the night they would smoke joints and exchange puerile Marxist analyses of the city's social problems. Their sex life came filtered through feminist assumptions about role and exploitation. Susan often felt she was being used. That made her angry. Rarely did she relax. How could she when sex was regarded as a political experience, not an emotional one?

A guru came ready-made in the form of a philosophy teacher. The instructor wasn't profound, although Susan wouldn't have been able to recognize profundity if it were dropped in her lap. He was good looking, captivating in class, and his view of "the good life" and "the good society" conformed to her own. That was enough. She idolized this man and dreamed

3

of leading the revolution as his Rosa (The Red) Luxemburg.

Her facile assumptions about people were confirmed by Rousseauvian tracts that she studied as though they were Talmudic texts. Man is basically a noble savage; there is an intrinsic decency to people; it is simply the "bad" institutions that corrupt "good" people.

Susan never asked herself who created those "bad" institutions. Her naive views of life hardened into an ideological posture. If people are basicly good, all one has to do with social misfits is allow their decency to rise to the surface through encouragement, assistance, concern and love. Where others failed, Susan was sure she could succeed.

As a way of testing her capacity to convert the bad institutions into sound ones, Susan devoted almost every minute of her free time to a social agency called Adopt-a-Building. This organization's mission was to restore abandoned and partially burned buildings to a condition approaching their original state.

Susan threw herself into the renovation of a building on the Lower East Side. She wrote proposals for federal money to finance repairs, cajoled friends into moving there, hired a superintendent and, to demonstrate that she wasn't a "liberal hypocrite," moved in herself. She painted and cleaned her pad so that it would be the house model. And she gave the garbage cans two coats of paint they had never had before.

When she talked about the project, she glowed. Although her family and friends thought she was mired in depression, she claimed she was "never happier." After all, the building proved that the city could work if people really cared, she contended. The building did work. There was a nursery in the basement, a meeting room used most often by women's groups that Susan liked, and 12 comfortable and comparatively clean apartments. It wasn't UN Plaza, but neither was it the kind of decaying building that usually serves for housing on the Lower East Side.

To celebrate the building's success Susan convinced the tenants to throw a house party that spring. There was a lot of wine, some joints and more than enough gaiety to go around. The tenants knew something special was happening in that building.

During the party the superintendent, who was one of Susan's reclamation projects, made a pass.

The man had an arrest record that included assault
and rape, but Susan... saw in him only another potential.
convert. She had hired him over the objection of
several tenants and, until the party, considered
her decision a good one. But he didn't take her
rejection well. Visibly angry, he left the room
and vowed to get revenge. No one took him seriously.
"Just the wine talking," said one of the tenants.

By the time the party was over and everyone
had cleared out, Susan could barely make her way
across the room to her convertible bed. There was
a race between approaching sleep and her desire
to get her clothes off. Sleep won.

At 4 AM the superintendent entered her room
with a pass key. He had been drinking heavily.
Without the slightest warning he raped and stabbed
her. She was dead within minutes. This was his
revenge for her decency.

The police heard her shrieks and were on the
scene instantly. In a moment of sobriety the superintendent admitted his crime. But the admission
could not bring back the young woman whose trust
was too fragile for the world.

Susan's idealism ran headlong into reality,
and reality triumphed. The goodness in man may

exist but it certainly didn't exist in this man.

On a sunny day in Utica the one synagogue was filled to overflowing for the funeral. Residents from all over town came to pay their last respects and to ask why. What conceivable explanation could account for the murder of a girl so young and so idealistic? The rabbi spoke of her social commitment. Susan , he said, would have selected the same path if she could start all over.

The words were well meant, but they just couldn't capture the truth of Susan's experience. For her life and her death severely tested '60s idealism. And the result for the spirit of the decade - and for Susan - was death at an early age.

CHAPTER 4

WHAT'S WRONG WITH A LITTLE PERFECTION?

There was a time not so long ago when cleanliness was next to Godliness, conscience was a good -
if at times constraining - influence and guilt was
a way of maintaining some social order. These views,
however, in the hang-loose era in which we live
are as anachronistic as Puritan values in Las Vegas.
In an attempt to justify the new social order, contemporary priests (read: psychiatrists) have labeled
people who live according to fixed, orderly principles as obsessive-compulsives, an appellation that
has the fury of psychiatric mumbo-jumbo behind it.
What if I do emphasize perfection in my own behavior?
Is it wrong to accept inelastic principles?

According to Dr. Leonard Crammer, a New York
psychiatrist and author of FREEDOM FROM COMPULSION,
there are many people who are uptight, neurotic
about moral inhibitions and overly concerned about
fulfilling obligations conscientiously. The cure
is simple: relax. Live with problems and "simply
assume that if the worst happens, I'll pay the price,
along with everyone else."

To test ourselves and make sure we are not one
of the uptight types, Crammer has devised an obsess-
ive-compulsive personality inventory that permits
self-rating. Several of the values on this scale

reveal a great deal about what Dr. Crammer considers
appropriate behavior at this time: "I get upset
if I don't finish a task"; "I like everything I
do to be perfect"; "I do things precisely to the
last detail"; "I plan my time so that I won't be
late"; "It bothers me when my surroundings are not
clean and tidy"; "I think that I expect worthy moral
standards in others"; "I think that I am sexually
inhibited"; "I find myself working rather than relax-
ing"; "I like to budget myself carefully and live
on a cash and carry basis."

According to the scoring, if we adhere to these
values none or a little or some of the time, it
is better than adhering to them a good part or most
of the time. If one extrapolates from this scoring
system and makes assumptions about the values therein,
it appears as if non-completion is better than completion of a task; imperfection is better than perfection; lateness is better than promptness; sloppi-
ness is better than tidiness; avoiding obligations
is better than fulfilling them; expecting moral
standards in others is worse than not expecting
them; promiscuity is better than sexual inhibition;
relaxation is better than work; being social is
better than being private; and being profligate

2

is better than being thrifty.

Of course, Dr. Crammer would disagree with this contention. But if one is "uptight, insecure and driving hard," the answer is "to ease off," which translates into relaxation of the values.

From my point of view, this attitude reflects another of the many assaults on traditional bourgeois values that the community of psychologists has launched. By assuming that we should live with problems, i.e., adjust to them, the implicit concern and probable effect is complacency. Don't worry about doing a better job, relax and enjoy yourself. Presumably enjoyment should be encouraged at the risk of jeopardizing hard work, effort, obligations and morality. In the process, the beneficiary will be less neurotic. What is ignored by Dr. Crammer and by far too many of his colleagues is the effect this relaxed attitude has on the society.

According to Freudian analysis, some degree of personal expression must be sacrificed in order to meet the demands of civilization. The price an individual pays for living in a stable society may be some degree of neurosis, a neurosis that is characterized by restraint on libidinal expression. The trade-off in bourgeois culture is social stability

and personal rewards for the maintenance of respect-
able principles, despite the limitation this might
impose on individual freedom.

This social contract that has been the essence
of bourgeois culture for 400 years is being eroded
by a combination of forces bent on expanding individual expression and eliminating traditional standards
of behavior. In the vanguard of what can now be
characterized as a movement are the psychologists,
particularly those who describe adherence to traditional principles as social pathology.

"Feel good about yourself," "don't worry so
much about commitments" are the admonitions to a
society that has been described as abnormal for
believing - or is it having believed? - in delayed
gratification, the imperfectiveness of human beings
and the observance of commitments. The new order
encourages us to act for any purpose whatever, so
long as we don't feel uptight and do feel relaxed.

In the extreme, one can envision a social system
that promotes anarchic behavior with the only concern
being the feeling of self-worth, regardless of the
acts committed. "It isn't bad that I don't work,
it's bad that I can't relax and enjoy the free time."
"It isn't the crime that's bad, but whether I feel

4

guilty about it." Standards in this scenario are
based on whim. This is psychological existentialism
gone wild.

All that I can hope for is that when crime is
even more prevalent than at present, when the garbage isn't collected, when the arrival of mail is
based on the astrological tables, when every decision
is based on feelings, that guilt may be reintroduced
as nourishing for the survival of civilization,
even if we become a little neurotic.

CHAPTER 5

TELEVISION REALITY

For many of us who considered television programming a vast wasteland, sports was the lush island
of the uncontrived surrounded by a polluted sea
of the synthetic. Even when the game was one-sided,
I'd sit glued to my screen as the final seconds ticked
away. When I thought about my addiction - which
wasn't often - I realized that the reason for my
gravitational pull to athletic events was their spontaneous reality. O. J. Simpson barreling down the
sidelines like a juggernaut was real. No matter
how jaundiced my opinions, they could not have been
so degraded by television's pseudoevents that I'd
lose O.J.'s reality - or so I believed.

In the past few years, however, a curious contest
between the real and the pseudosports event has emerged. Admittedly, I can still watch O.J.'s magical
moves through the line; but competing with my image
of this football star is a new montage of O.J. riding
a bicycle on "Superstars," hitting a forehand on
"Celebrity Tennis" and leaping hurdles for the Hertz
Corporation. And I find myself outraged that one
of the last vestiges of television reality is strug-
gling to survive. I feel I've been let down - the
event is rigged, and I've been enticed by the appearance of my heroes, who masquerade as media celebrities.

What possible relationship is there between tennis competition and the pomp accompanying the "Love Doubles"? Even the title suggests a soap opera rather than a tennis match. What possible concern can the viewer have for Dave Kingman's weight-lifting feats? I want to see him hit home runs. Who cares how well Jerry West does in HORSE against a female basketball player? I want to see him hit 20-foot jump shots against the Celtics.

One doesn't have to be an aficionado to distinguish between the authentic and inauthentic events. The latter's hype has no boundaries of good taste and propitiousness. "The Love Doubles" appeal relied as heavily on the on-again off-again Evert-Conners romance as on the tennis skills of the protagonists. Should one really care whether Elke Sommer has a good serve or whether Desi Arnez, Jr., knows the difference between "deuce" and "your advantage"? Are there many football fans who really care what the Friars have to say about Joe Namath? In fact, Namath has been so immersed in his inauthentic roles that he appears to have forgotten how he became a celebrity in the first place.

With its power to magnify, television is capable of taking the few remaining sports heroes and blowing

them up into clebrities. Any athlete who is overexposed - and every good athlete is overexposed -
is subject to the flashy and usually ephemeral life
of the television personality. Johnny Carson expects
Hank Aaron to describe his home run hitting skills
in three minutes, or before commercial intervention;
while Wilt Chamberlain is expected to stand next
to Bob Hope and draw cheap laughs because of his
size.

These heroes of sport, who not only preoccupied
every waking moment of my teen years but also represented my values, are not mere illusions manufactured
like cellophane. Once they achieve a reputation,
it is seemingly unimportant how they appear, just
so long as they do appear. Producers sell program
with personalities, even if in the process Namath
is reduced to a third-rate comedian, Willie Mays
to a car salesperson and Joe DiMaggio to a bank tell-
er. Why should Mark Spitz's unprecedented seven
Olympic gold medals for swimming automatically qualify him as a TV pitchman?

Even the Olympic events, which represent the best
tradition in sports and for which television coverage
is sometimes quite good, are contaminated by pre-
liminary events, programs on the personalities and

3

extraneous material that becloud reality. Why am
I forced to know more about Dorothy Hamill than the
fact that she is a gifted skater? Does it add to
her reputation if I am told that she's from Hamden,
Connecticut, always wanted to skate backwards and
her parents are divorced? By making preliminaries
important, by dimming my recollection of memorable
sports moments and by offering information I cannot
digest, the illusions challenge and erode the truth.
The heroic and the memorable are reduced to half-
recalled images whose stature approaches yesterday's
news. But if we sports addicts don't like what's
happening, what can we do and to whom do we do it?

In an effort to discover the bogeymen and their
motives, I spoke with sports department officials
at ABC and CBS. The ABC official described "Superstars" as "entertainment," not as a sports program.
He indicated - to my surprise, I might add - that
"ABC is philosophically opposed to contrived events."
However, philosophical predilections are often subordinated to righ ratings; and "Superstars," with
an audience of 17 million viewers, has excellent
ratings. Thus, the program not only stays on the
air, its progeny emerge as television specials.
"Superstars" has given birth to "Team Superstars"

4

[an event in which the Super Bowl teams compete with one another], "Women Superstars" and "Celebrity Super-stars." Obviously, the formula is finally terminated when - and only when - the ratings decline.

CBS officials defended "Challenge of the Sexes" as a liberating program for female athletes, a way of encouraging a female audience for weekend sports. It makes little difference that "Challenge of the Sexes" is an attempt to capitalize on the popularity of the Women's Movement, even if what pretends to be sports competition is largely entertainment.

What is clear at two of the three major networks is the influence of game-show entertainment on sports programming. It is not that the network sports di-rectors are merely venal; on the contrary, they honestly believe themselves to be responsive. But they ignore the effect television programming has in influencing taste. While directors comment about the ratings, they seem conspicuously ignorant of the subtle way in which TV programming overshadows our ability to discriminate. How can one discriminate when pseudo-events are more exciting than the real thing? Every CBS Las Vegas tennis match becomes "the match of the century to determine the world's greatest player." There are no casual encounters. We have been so besieged with superlatives that anything less than the "greatest" isn't worth our attention. In the process, we are not only unaware of what's "good," we **are unable** to discern what is authentic.

Perhaps the influence of the contrived event is inexorable. Perhaps the medium lends itself to this kind of expression. But I can vividly recall Bobby Thomson's home run, Robby dancing off first, a Dr. J. dunk, a circus catch by Lynn Swann and a Bobby Orr power play appearing on my television screen as graphically as life. I know in my gut what these events are. And I also know how different much of what constitutes contemporary sports programming is. My fear is that illusion will replace the actual so quickly that even those sports freaks who still retain the power of discrimination will be unable to make a last stand for reality.

CHAPTER 6

IT'S ALL SHOW BIZ

Calvin Coolidge once said: "The business of America is business." For 40 years, this was unquestionably true; the business ethos dominated cultural attitudes whether the area of concern was trends in fashion or literature. Economic and commercial values were preeminent. One could reject or embrace American business but one certainly couldn't ignore it.

John Dos Passos, in U.S.A., used business activities as a perennial cloud hanging over his main characters' lives, just as Homer employed the gods on Mount Olympus to determine the fate of Hector and Achilles. But in the age of electronic wizardry, where soft drinks are sold with musical comedy routines, one wonders if this notion of business style is at all applicable. In this age, it is probably appropriate to argue that the business of America is show business.

There was a time, not very long ago, when institutional purpose was easily defined: the churches were concerned with religion; athletes with sports; politicians with politics. That idea, however, has been locked away with the relics of another era.

What are we to make of a former President who offers Bob Hope the "Peoples Choice" award on a nationally televised program? Is this politics, building good will, offering a well-deserved award to a national figure or virtually undisguised show-manship? Who cares whether Willie Mays delivers a joke well on the Mike Douglas Show? Is the view of Episcopal priests on lesbianism of any significance other than the fact that church officials are perplexed about their public posture?

At a time when show business is what counts, athletes sign contracts which stipulate **how often** their picture will appear on the cover of game programs. Politicians use their public personæ to secure jobs as newscasters. And church officials are in the vanguard of radical social reform movements.

It is not simply the confusion in role to which I object, but the style that makes this confusion so palpable. To reach the public - it is often alleged - by the Mad. Ave. types - one must reduce all complex arguments to the level of the 30-second commercial.

"Network" demonstrates in its crass way that the news is show business, in fact any view - the more bizarre the better - that generates a significant audience rating is show business. If Karl Marx could humorously explain Das Kapital on the Johnny Carson

2

Show, he would be eligible for an Emmy. And the Emmy Awards would probably garner a fantastic (only superlatives will do) audience share, if Marx should receive his award from President Carter by saying: "I'd like to thank you, the enemies of the state and all those enlightened proletarians who listened to me on the Johnny Carson Show. Proletarians of the world unite, you have nothing to lose but your views. And what difference does that make anyway – NBC has marvelous views for you. Let me also thank my collaborator, Frederick Engels, whose assistance made this all possible. And last, but not least, let me thank my bourgeois, narrowly Jewish parents who inspired my rebellion and resentment."

If this seems strikingly impossible - and it is - consider the international awards won by Godard for his soporific films that do little more than propagandize audiences with puerile Marxist dogma and then are acclaimed at the Cannes film festival by thousands of adoring, bourgeois critics who have discovered the "hidden meaning" in his unintelligible scripts. In this case, politics is show business because of the medium selected for the message.

For someone to be a public figure he/she must be conspicuously lacking in seriousness and willing

3

to embrace show business deportment. For example,
it is as imperative for former Mayor Landsay to maintain a **tan, ap**pear on network television shows and
be seen in the company of rock groups as to understand issues. In fact as a result of the show business demands, symbols are often more important than
issues.

CHAPTER 7

THE VANISHING ATHLETIC HERO

If my reading of Chip Hilton stories at the age of 12 was any guide, I would argue that we have seen the last of the athletic hero. In this period of journalistic hyperbole one can find superstars and great - even "the greatest" - sports luminaries basking in the glow of publicity, but heroes cannot be found. For the hero, I am convinced, is an extinct species relegated to the memory of my youthful idealism.

The hero was not necessarily the one who hit the winning home run in the last of the ninth or the one who scored the winning basket at the buzzer. He was the teammate capable of the extraordinary sacrifice.

He was Lou Gehrig, who played with dignity while his body struggled to recall what it once did instinctively. He was Jackie Robinson, who turned the other cheek even when he was filled with rage. He was Willis Reed, playing on one leg because the team needed his presence on the court. The hero controlled his ego because he knew that his action would benefit his teammates.

The Athlete's Narcissism

In baseball, the sacrifice is now performed almost exclusively by marginal players, while the

cleanup hitters are trying to go downtown on every
swing. Yet in the 1940's and 50's, Jackie Robinson,
the cleanup hitter on a great hitting club, led the
team in sacrifices almost every year he played. Despite the rhetoric of team play, how many basketball
players ignore personal statistics for the benefit
of the team? How many football players prefer
anonymity rather than the spotlight of television
and Hollywood?

Some, who have recognized this condition, blame
it on big-money contracts predicated on performance
(read: statistics). Others argue that it is the
glamour of the media that affects action on the field.
Instant celebrities are made on Monday Night Football.
But I think that while these factors contribute,
the hero has disappeared because of the athlete's
narcissism.

Sport has become an arena for peacocks who display
their colors for the edification of television producers. Style has replaced sacrifice because that's
what attracts attention. Cool Clyde may have style,
but ask Paul Westphal how difficult (or how easy)
it is to drive by him. Broadway Joe may have a lot
of women, but ask opposing defensive backs if they
fear his passes. Reggie may be selling millions

of candy bars, but ask Luis Tiant if a changeup won't
have Reggie swinging four feet in front of the pitch.

Heroes might have loved publicity; they unquestionably coveted money and fame. But in most cases
they made a distinction between what would lead to
personal aggrandizement and what was best for the
team.

When Ted Williams in 1941 had achieved his goal
of batting .400, he could have sat out the second
game of a doubleheader and been assured of retaining
this average. But he insisted on playing in the
second game, even if it jeopardized the mark he had
reached. He played because he did not want to back
into .400, but his gesture at least had the appearance of sacrifice.

Now even the appearances are gone. It is player
against player. There is even competition for photo-
graphs on the cover of a program. Most basketball
teams want to play with five basketballs to keep
their superstars content. Baseball stars argue with
their managers if they aren't batting in one of the
glamour spots in the lineup: third, fourth or fifth.

The stars also have to look the part. It isn't
enough to throw touchdowns or score baskets; now
one must smell sexy, wear clothes like Beau Brummel,

comb one's hair like Warren Beatty and smile like
Liberace. If most of the stars spent as much time
practicing their game as looking in the mirror, the
quality of our games would improve and so might the
athlete's image.

But this won't happen. This is the age of the
superstar, not the hero. And superstars specialize
in self-adulation, not sacrifice.

CHAPTER 8
BEVERLY HILLS CHIC

For easterners not used to Beverly Hills, it never ceases to surprise us. The conspicuous spending surpasses anything from Seal Harbor to Coconut Grove. The emphasis on cars would make Detroit rejoice, except that no one drives an American-made car. And the gaucherie is startling even for those who were nurtured by the nouveau riche of Long Island.

There is no question that the world of Hollywood images has intruded on the area where the stars reside. This, of course, is only partially true since many of the stars have long since migrated south to La Jolla, Newport Beach and Laguna, leaving Beverly Hills to aerospace executives. But it doesn't matter. The stars left behind a style fostered by public relation blurbs, excessive income and a keeping up with the Gable and Grable psychology. Almost everyone who lives in Beverly Hills is touched by the glow of stardom.

Several weeks ago my wife and I went to Beverly Hills to visit some friends who are in the television business. After passing the fading pink facade of the Beverly Hills Hotel, we made a left on Beverly Drive and proceeded up Coldwater Canyon Drive. The road was lined with alternating tall and medium sized palm trees that stood straight and exact, although they didn't have any of the brown stain I have come to expect on palm leaves.

There were no people on the street; no one sitting on a front porch rocker, no kids riding bikes or even skateboards. The new homes combined colonial columns with a monolithic marble entrance or Spanish gates and Bauhaus functionalism. Paradoxes abound.

As soon as we met our friends, I knew something had changed. Six months in the land of stars had its effect. I was greeted with a cool hello known in California as the "laid-back attitude" (if I hear that expression one more time I'll fall asleep). "What's running down, now?" "Running down?" I asked myself. The meaning was clear enough, but all I could think of was jogging downhill.

This over-fifty teenager was in the land of mellow and he had imbibed Beverly Hills chic the way Woody Allen digested the idioms of Flatbush. His sunglasses were large enough to hide his face completely. But what was concealed on his face was revealed on his chest. Curly gray hairs nestled out of a skin-tight silk shirt. They were so well curled that the mountain breeze didn't seem to affect their alignment. His pants were off-white linen, string tied and fashionably baggy. Of course, there

2

were no socks under his white Bally loafers.

The first urgent matter that we discussed –
that was unquestionably not laid back - was the pur-
chase of a car, not any car, mind you, but a 1973
Corvette, the last year a conventional convertible
was manufactured. "Later models have that awful
'T-bar' across the top that simply destroys the line."
I was duly impressed, although I didn't realize the
bar "destroyed the line." Cars in Beverly Hills
are like brains. They determine where you go to
school, who your friends will be and even what attitudes you have.

At one party a fellow said, "The car you buy
is a function of your personality." Immediately
I knew I was in trouble. I don't own a car and the
last car I had was a Ford Fairlane. According to
this equation either I had no personality or I was
a Fairlane. "People who drive a Rolls or Bentley
are important," he noted as heads nodded in recognition. I sat there incredulously, but the lesson
was only beginning.

The following day we decided to window shop
on Rodeo Drive, the Mecca for those who are shopping
to be seen. As I drove my Hertz Co. Toyota to a
parking lot, a young man dressed in a red crushed

3

velvet tuxedo that was as inappropriate as a mink coat in Miami, snidely asked, "Do you want to park that thing here?" This Toyota heard many of my cuss words when it refused to start one morning, but it had never before been described as a "thing." Offended but undaunted I calmly said "Yes, park this thing next to the Porsche - maybe something will rub off."

By then I understood the rules of the Beverly Hills game. This parking valet had learned from experience that a Rolls driver gave him a $5 tip, while he was lucky to get 50 cents from the Toyota driver. In my case he was wrong - I only gave him a quarter. His look of dismay suggested that his stereotype of Toyotas and their owners or renters was reinforced.

Rodeo Drive is a testimonial to the slogan of "acquisitions at any price." It made the boutiques on upper Madison Avenue appear as Orchard Street bargain havens. Not knowing very much about the shops my wife suggested that I pick out a Father's Day present for myself. It wasn't very hard to do.

There was a stylish cotton shirt that appealed to my beachwear fantasies. Without any hesitation I told a beautiful sales mannequin that, "I'll take

4

that one." She proceeded to wrap it and then asked
for my charge card. Since I figured it probably
cost $30 I said, "I'll pay for it in cash." With-
out flinching she said, "That will be $179 plus tax."
Sheepishly I repeated the number in the expectation
that it would change. In 20 seconds we disappeared
from that counter without my Father's Day present
vowing that this would indeed by a window-shopping
venture.

The price of everything in Beverly Hills is
at least three times its real value. That is part
of the style. Since nothing is worth what you pay
for it, purchasers have a surreal quality to them.
Houses are discussed in the millions of dollars,
film properties in the tens of millions and meals
in hundred dollar denominations. For me this simply
resembled a Monopoly game with Sunset Boulevard sub-
stituting for Park Place and Boardwalk. The big
difference, however, is that I felt as if I lost
$200 every time I passed Sunset instead of collecting
that sum for passing Boardwalk.

For tourists, Beverly Hills chic is best characterized now by the sheik's house on Sunset Boulevard. His statues resemble Hals' nudes in finger
paint colors. The flowers in huge ornate vases are

plastic and the stone pieces in the exterior wall
resemble linoleum chips. From the huge fountain
to the green paint the house is grotesque. Yet it
is also a comment, however unwitting, on the area.
Plastic is in; tasteful is out. The house is a monu-
ment to fatuous standards.

Irate Beverly Hills residents have denounced
the sheik and his style. Yet his palace is only
an extreme version of the architecture to be found
in Bel Air and Truesdale a couple of miles away.
In a sense, this Arab has held up a mirror to the
residents of the star city who are forced to look
at themselves every time they drive along Sunset
Boulevard. They may not like what they see, but this
caricature is only possible because of the already
present Beverly Hills style.

Beverly Hills chic can most easily be discerned
in sentences that begin with the phrase, "My psychic
says..." Ears perk up as if E.F. Hutton himself was
about to give us a stock selection. After all, the
psychic knows what we can only guess. He lives in
the transcendent world of future actions. What
better sources does one require to plan a future?

Dozens of jean-clad, open-shirted, clog-supported
men and their much younger female counterparts will

be transfixed by the claims of psychic gurus who have - by their own admission - broken the barriers of the unknown. The psychic will be called for business decisions, issues of love and where to go for a restful vacation.

Beverly Hills chic can also be noticed through the wandering it encourages. People simply wander from one house to another. There is no special rhyme or reason to this wanderlust, except that it helps to pass the day. For someone unaccustomed to this practice, it can be unnerving. "Who are you?" I said to one unannounced wanderer. "Me? Why, I'm the guy who always passes through. How's it going?" I couldn't tell him. But I could tell him to keep his movement in forward gear.

When one does have a conversation the topic usually is weight. "Hey, I'm down to 155," or "With this diet, I dropped ten in a week." It all sounds like the betting board at Las Vegas. If weight isn't discussed then jogging is. "I'm up to two miles; now that I've reached that goal I'm working on my aerobics." It was amusing to think of these short-legged, unathletic television executives preparing for what had become the Beverly Hills marathon run. But there they were! Head gear from Head to Tretorn sneakers - a picture of swagger in motion.

It was curious that from day one of our trip to departure seven days later, no one mentioned a book. We saw exquisite gun collections, visited three-million-dollar houses, ate a very average but magnificently priced meal at Chasen's, jogged at a local "jogging park," spent time at a set, but did not hear one word about or even see one person read a book. Surely people in Beverly Hills must read, even if it's only THE THORNBIRDS. Yet there appears to be a conspicuous avoidance of the printed word. This is the land of electronic media. If McLuhan is a charlatan in New York, he is a genuine guru in Beverly Hills.

We said goodbye to our friends as they whispered some mystical allusions about happiness they probably heard from the psychic. On our way to the airport we drove by the sheik's place as gawkers smiled at the tasteless display of ugly statues and garish decor. We watched the parade of Rolls Royces, Bentleys, Ferraris, Maseratis and Porsches on Sunset Boulevard. We shook our heads in bemused silence as the joggers passed us by. And we listened carefully as friends exchanged mellow greetings about what was running down.

New York may be the pits for these Beverly Hills

residents. It may be in debt to the top of the World Trade Center. It may be humid and hot and the subways may seal the smell of perspiration below the surface. But after Beverly Hills chic all I could think of was, "New York here I come, right back where I started from." It was hokey alright; that's probably why we laughed so hard.

CHAPTER 9
WHAT'S GOOD AS I SEE IT, IS WHAT'S GOOD

At a recent lecture at New York University on contemporary art the lecturer was asked, "How do you know whether the work is good?" Somewhat taken aback, the lecturer responded, "If the work is creative." Still perplexed, the student countered, "But how do you determine what's creative?" With much less hesitation this time, the lecturer said, "In modern art creativity can be equated with novelty."

Those words were indelibly etched in my brain: "Creativity equals novelty." The meaning is bizarre, albeit revealing. In order to be creative, presumably one must do something different. Here is the latest social justification for doing your own thing. Whether the artist demonstrates skill, discipline and knowledge is unimportant. What does count is whether his work is different. With this kind of relativist interpretation the normative dimensions of the good and beautiful are reduced to personal whim.

What happened to standards? Where are those consensual values that determine artistic taste? And how does one decide what is good and bad? In a world of impermanence and novelty artistic standards that had legitimacy for the design of a cultural conception are gone. As Henry James noted in his

famous passage on taste, cultural standards are hard
to obtain and, by implication, harder to maintain:

"...it takes an endless amount of history
to make even a little tradition, and an
endless amount of tradition to make even a
little taste, and an endless amount of taste,
by the same token, to make even a little
tranquility."

The idea of continuous change that characterizes
the cultural world is divorced from the past, impa-
tient with tradition, lacking in taste, bewildering
in conception and tumultuous in its results. What
James admonished against is with us. Culture doesn't
mitigate change and serve as a symbol of order and
continuity in which people can find repose. It is
the bellweather of change and vicissitudes; it's
"what's happening." A universal standard of art
has been replaced by the personal standard of prefer-
ence. "If I think it's good, it therefore must be
good." This self-indulgence that challenges consensus
at every turn now masquerades as artistic criticism.
And the art world, in its desire to accommodate this
opinion, makes ever more elaborate gestures to form
and style while substance is ignored. Although
a host of factors probably account for this phenomenon,

2

including most obviously the erosion of universal social standards, there are particular reasons that I believe are the culprits in this examination: revolutionary politics; a loss of identity and artistic freedom.

The revolutionary fervor of our times demands the spread of a world-immanent gospel through the arts. Politicize culture, so the argument suggests, and you help politicize people. As a result only social-political statements in the arts are proffered as noble. The great masters are condemned as "reactionary" because their work produces quiet joy and catharsis instead of fostering the "sense of injur'd merit" and inciting the revolutionary appetite. In this way traditional standards are initiated by the "new standard" of the social-political aesthetic: Propaganda becomes confused with artistic expression and the compassion, kindness, tact and discipline that so represent the work of classical artists is seen as "escapism" and "decadence."

As the nation is increasingly concerned about who and what it is, it stands to reason that one manifestation of that dilemma is the loss of identity, a phrase that is overused and poorly understood. Restlessly in search of a belief system that is for-

3

ever undermined, Americans look to their culture
for answers. But that culture is a mirror of prevailing values; and the one value that remains constant is a belief in change. The result is the mutually contradictory values of change as a reflection
of principles in the marketplace and "standards"
as that cluster of ideas that require stability,
continuity and identity. The conditions of cultural
standards that rest on the value of stable ends for
their contribution to the quality of life are at
odds with the utilitarian principle of temporary
goals for commercial enrichment.

The contemporary critic has come to assume that
artistic creativity is perforce a function of freedom
above all else. For the artist, freedom of expression
is indeed imperative, but as Proust, among others,
has pointed out, there is the prerequisite of discipline . An artist who has nothing but his freedom
has the means to create but not the vision for crea-
tion. Andre Gide put the matter even more cogently
by noting that "Art is born of discipline and dies
of freedom." In the contemporary art world, these
dangers are realities. Anyone free to express himself is an artist whether he has a discipline or
not. And the freedom so treasured by the culture

4

has deteriorated into artistic anarchy that values
only the ephemeral.

A personal view of culture that makes one
opinion as good as any other ultimately leads to
no standards at all. That is the course we are on.
In this case - as in so many others - real progress
must take the form of recovery. We must recover
those transcendent values that give meaning to cultural works. To do something notable in this age
is to find the means whereby contemporary critics
and observers of the arts can be made to rediscover
standards, which not very long ago were jealously
guarded truths.

Chapter 10

THE GATEWAY TO PRE-TEEN SEXUALITY

A convoy of pre-pubescent girls moved very slowly along Hempstead Turnpike on their way to an altar of sexual initiation. For this day in the beginning of March marked the fulfillment of the pre-teen dream: a chance to see and hear Shaun Cassidy at the Nassau Coliseum.

Falsely advertised as a concert, this was a rite of sexual fantasy designed to titillate impressionable female psyches.

Cassidy did not disappoint his followers. He began his act by performing gyrations behind a paper screen. His silhouette moving frantically to the beat of the drums and the thunderous shrieks of girls left limp by their own exhortations.

Then - in what was symbolically an ideal way to commence his singing - he burst through the paper ring that had concealed his tiny frame and continued this sexual metaphor with his hit song "Caroline Is Coming."

For his admirers it had the tingling affect of alcohol in an open wound.

The songs from his albums have as much sophistication as a grunt. They purport to be bubblegum and unquestionably are. Even those tunes borrowed from the Beatles and Ronettes sounded like love sick sighs that breathlessly leave the stomach lining so that there is room for popcorn and coke.

Wearing Fry boots, jeans rolled up neatly to the top of the boot and military shirts that reveal the campaigns in which they've engaged, the pre-teens emulate the attire of their teen-age models, but Shaun Cassidy hero worship is idiosyncratically part of their cohort group.

This is a generation of Hardy Boys freaks who have come to admire the androgynous appearance of male media stars. To be cut is to be epicene.

Cassidy's dress and appearance suggest he understands what turns the pre-teen on. Wearing a blue sequin halter top, white satin pants stretched over his tiny rear end, hair that has all the signs of a short Farrah Fawcett Majors permanent and a tee shirt, he seems like the American flag of pre-teen aspirations.

He made the most of his outfit. First he would remove his halter as if he had his early show business training in strip shows. Then he would turn his back to the audience wiggling his rear furiously. He would pump and grind, split and move, jump and hop as his pelvis was in perpetual motion.

Meanwhile parents - of which I was one - sat mildly bemused or simply bored. I kept asking myself how promoters could take a youth with so little talent and parley him into a multi million dollar commodity.

The answer is fairly apparent. Sell sex. Make it palatable for parents, innocent enough for pre-teens and subtle enough for the media; but let the message get across.

Shaun Cassidy is the latest in a long line of pre-teen idols, including his step brother, who are the rage of ten year olds with purchasing power that should not be underestimated. These pre-teens buy records, convince Dad that in order to be dutiful he must shell out $8.50 for a concert ticket, put expensive posters in their rooms and watch television programs. Their taste - to the extent they have any - translate into what Madison Avenue now calls megabucks.

Shaun Cassidy is a megabuck production. He un-wittingly represents the standard of a commercial culture that exploits teen-age sexual fantasies with expensive rites of passage. A program at his concert costs $4.00; tee shirts go for three and orange sodas are 65¢. This is a very expensive substitute for masturbation.

Yet we are trapped by the existential demands of the age. One cannot isolate a child from kitch; parents, no matter how resourceful, cannot dictate taste. We can only hope that Shaun Cassidy represents a pre-adolescent phase, a time when innocence is partially preserved. But I speak for parents when I say that I've been taken. Placed in the dilemma of damned if I do, damned if I don't, I resent the options but see no way out. Contemporary society is relentless in its insidious sale of popular culture. When Shaun Cassidy sighs, "Hey Deenie won't you come out tonight" the pre-teen passions surface and parents are caught in the grip of a commercial gravitation that is inescapable.

CHAPTER 1
HOW I LEARNED TO RESPECT THE POLICE

As a boy, I used to put on the policeman's cap I was given as a birthday present and daydream about catching a thief. I was preserving law and order against the onslaught of criminal offenders. "John Dillinger stick'em up, ya under arrest." I never really outgrew these fantasies, although, as I was passing through a postadolescent Marxist phase in my life, the police became the enemy. That was very temporary, however, a little like the period when I believed that I would be president of the U.S.

In the 1960's, my affection for policemen was rediscovered. Despite what I read about police brutality at Columbia and Berkeley, I observed an extraordinary degree of self-restraint and professional behavior exhibited by the police under the most trying circumstances. How would you like to be called "pig" by hundreds of angry teenagers for doing your assigned job or have dog feces thrown at you for asking some ersatz Lenin to take his feet off the university president's desk?

As a police sympathizer, my passions may have been with the law officers, but as an academic I discussed criminal matters with all the dispassion a scholar can muster. My students, of course, did not appreciate the dispassionate analysis and actively resisted the passionate claims. However, I did admit that my experience was limited and my arguments were distillations of secondary sources. That was something I lamented, but, no matter what I wished, my childish daydreams remained unfulfilled and my knowledge vicarious.

This condition was to change more quickly than I could have imagined. It started when the New York Council of the Humanities funded a project to have humanists (academics, journalists, and religious leaders) ride with police officers and discuss police issues. I was selected as one of these humanists. Unbeknownst to my benefactors, I was secretly longing to sacrifice my books for a patrol car. What I craved was to be a knight in blue, fulfilling atavistic yearnings.

What Reporters Fail To Discuss

The police, I discovered, are not what my daydreams were about, nor are they the sensational subjects most newspaper reporters tend to highlight. They are unquestionably caught in the maelstrom of urban decay they did not create. They have an impossible job that the citizenry generally does not understand and is often unwilling to support. Now that the obvious is noted, it should be pointed out that most of these men are brave and decent, although some simply do "the job" and a small number are psychopathic and brutal. It amazes me that some policemen can say "I'll make a collar at 11:00 p.m." and do it every time. Is that chance or a result of the use of provocation to bolster one's arrest record?

What is also interesting is that, while most reporters discuss the stress on the job, few realize that the stress police complain about most emanates from petty and arbitrary decisions made by commanders and absurd decisions made by politicians who use the crime problem for their own purposes.

These random thoughts were not learned through a couple of scatter-shot visits to the Bronx [one of the five boroughs of New York City , my assigned area - I worked with a team in the Bronx Taskforce and rode in their patrol car for 40 hours over a two-month period. Admittedly, that does not qualify me as an expert, albeit John Kenneth Galbraith knows less about China than I know about the Bronx and that certainly did not stop him from writing a book about the subject.

My first day at the Bronx Taskforce office was revealing. The officers in this unit think of themselves as an elite command that has the mobility to address any trouble spot in the borough. The

esprit is obvious. A pastel drawing of a skull and

crossbones with a police cap serves as the unit sym-

bol. The walls have [New York] DAILY NEWS headlines

with handwritten supplements: e.g., "The T.F. Cares

For The Aged"; "Keep the faith, make a collar today."

There are statistics of arrests from Jan. 1 to the

present. The conversation is sprinkled with references

to children, being overweight, and an anticipated

softball game. An outsider would feel quite confi-

dent in asserting that these cops share some special

camaraderie.

I was assigned to two officers who have been

with the Taskforce for several years. They are sea-

soned professionals and as easy to talk to as anyone

I have ever known. Despite some initial apprehension

about their response to me, I actually looked forward

to our conversations as much as my chance to experi-

ence police work. These men could talk knowledgeably

about chess, child-rearing, pop music, Arthur Jensen's

theories of genetics and intelligence, Dr. J. [basket-

ball star Julius Erving], and police behavior. They

stared long and hard at well-built women and smiled

easily at children. They are not especially gung-

ho about their work, but, if we found ourselves in

a difficult situation, I was happy to know they were on my side.

Lessons of the Streets

They know the streets the way I know my classroom. Relatively trivial matters that might suggest something is awry were usually noticed. "I wonder why the birds are so active in that particular tree?" "Those kids don't look as if they belong on that school bus." They have street savvy that lets their minds filter events the way screens distinguish between sand and solid objects.

The fact that they are black is important. It was difficult to ride more than half a mile without their waving to someone they know. I often thought that half the Bronx must be related to these men. Moreover, by knowing and caring about so many, they become neighborhood cops in the only way that expression makes sense.

On my first day out, we rode through the 4-6, an area in transition that is feeling the cancerous effects of South Bronx sprawl. It is interesting that the South Bronx, which used to be the area between 130th and 138th Sts., now encompasses every part of the Bronx up to Yankee Stadium. Buildings with lovely facades are abandoned and mangy dogs

5

stand vigil in front of apartments that their owners
left months ago. This area combines some stable
families, the elderly — too poor to migrate to Miami,
and transients, who comprise the bulk of the criminal
element.

Fordham Rd., smack in the center of this pre-
cinct, is still a mecca for shoppers. Old women,
who have made a ritualistic walk along the Grand
Concourse till they reach the Bronx's most famous
bargain emporium, Alexander's Department Store, can
still be found with babushkas on their heads, rolled-
down Supphose stockings, and old woolen coats that
cover the calf. There is one striking difference,
however, between the past and now - fear. These
women are the bait for 14- and 15- year-old "juven-
iles" eager to make a fast buck. At times, these
teenagers use knives for their larceny, sometimes
a tug is sufficient, and some even employ attack
dogs. The effect is the same. Everyone is scared,
but the walkers are out because they would not know
what else to do with their lives.

As we were riding about four blocks south of
Fordham Rd. on what was a very peaceful day, "my
partners" (Scotty and Kenny) - I was obviously get-
ting deep into my role - stopped the car in front

of a street scene that included an unconscious woman,
a man trying to prop her up and occasionally slap
her into consciousness, and several very youthful
spectators. Scotty bent down over her, held her
hand gently, and mumbled some inaudible words. Mirac-
ulously , she woke up. Flailing at her boyfriend,
she shouted for all of the Bronx to hear that she
was the sister of the Black Jesus. That condition -
she alleged - had caused all her problems. It was
obvious that the woman was drugged and unquestionably
deranged.

We drove her to the hospital at breakneck speed
only after Scotty promised he would not leave her
side. She seemed to know every nurse at the hospital
and most of the doctors. "Where is Dr. Greenspan?"
she bellowed, "he's the only one who understands
me." The nurse asked Scotty about the case, but
all he said was "she should be detoxified." Apparently, if he claimed she required psychiatric assistance, he would have had to spend the entire day talking to psychiatrists before a decision about her
future would be made. It was far simpler to avoid
that issue.

After that scene, I started to understand the
policeman's role a little better. He is part social

worker, part psychologist, and peripherally a crime
fighter. When he is on the beat or parks his car,
he becomes a willy-nilly police department. He makes
decisions about when to arrest, when to ignore, and
when to assist. That kind of responsibility takes
its toll, especially when command decisions invariably resemble "Catch-22." For example, at one meeting, the men in the Taskforce were told to "keep
up the numbers" - translation: more arrests and
summonses. The same commander, however, said that
in Co-op City [a huge complex of high-rise apartment
houses, in itself larger than many U.S. cities] there
were to be no summonses given out at all. Now how
does a police officer "keep up the numbers" if he
is assigned to Co-op City? That kind of contradic--
tory direction has its effect. Moreover, if the newspapers discover an issue, so will the command. There
is no police initiative - the men are told to respond
to what the press has discovered. Crimes against
the elderly only became an issue when the NEW YORK
POST ran a special series on the matter. Experienced
officers can predict their assignments on the basis
of newspaper headlines.

Danger and Boredom

One Spring day, as Kenny, Scotty, and I were

involved in an animated conversation about the impending basketball playoffs, a well-dressed guy stopped the car on Westchester Ave. and angrily said, "Some kid holding a gun in his hand said he was goin' to blow my head off." He pointed in the direction the youth was walking. We drove quickly along Westchester Ave. in the wrong direction until we approached a male, 17-20 year-old who held what appeared to be a revolver in his right hand. Scotty and Kenny jumped out of the car in an instant. Kenny ran directly up to him from behind as Scotty negotiated his way around a row of parked cars. They moved like two football defensive backs, each compensating for the other's moves. I stood back, nervous about what would happen. Would the youth be "blown away"? Would he instinctively turn and start firing before Kenny reached him? I stood frozen for several seconds as adrenalin pumped through my body. When I next looked up, Kenny had his hand on the gun and the youth was disarmed. It turned out to be a plastic pistol.

"Did you know that was a toy gun?" I asked. "No," Kenny replied, "I simply wanted to close the distance between us as fast as possible. I didn't know that was a toy unil I got my hand on it." Kenny

and Scotty understand the street scene and one
another so well that their reaction time was phenom-
enal . Before my heartbeat could adjust to events,
the matter was over.

The danger in police activity is palpable. What
generally is not known - partly because of television
programming- is the sheer boredom of the job. Riding
in a squad car for eight hours on a day shift with
no reports from Central Headquarters can be deadly.
There are women to look at on the streets and talk
about their children's Little League game. There
is a rating system on female anatomy and Italian
pastry - anything to make the time go faster.

Occasionally, there is humor. In an area overheated with tension, that is one of the few releases.
On one tour, our car was hailed by a cab driver. In
a thick Yiddish accent, he told us that a woman was
trying to "stiff him" for $10. A Columbia University
professor had taken this cab from Manhattan to the
Bronx Veterans Hospital carrying only a $100 bill.
When she reached her destination and wanted to pay
the cabdriver with this bill, he went crazy. Having
all the insulation from life a university appointment
confers, she proceeded to a local bodega [Puerto
Rican grocery store] for change and was promptly

laughed out of the store as Spanish expletives
abounded. Finally, in desperation, she offered to
take the cabdriver to lunch so that she could get
change to pay him. This was all he had to hear.
"Vhat do I need a t'in broad like you, ven I have
a vonderful vife vaiting for me in Brooklyn. I didn't
come to de Bronx to get laid. I just vant my money.
Dere is someting wrong vit da air in de Bronx. Everyone's crazy." As my partners escorted the professor
to a local bank, I remained with the cabdriver. "I
vant you should arrest her," he demanded. "Now wait
a minute," I replied, "you're going to get your money."
"But I'm vasting my time in dis crazy area. Arrest
her!" "Let me explain something to you. I'm not
really a cop; I'm a police humanist working on a project in which I observe police behavior." That did
it - the cabdriver almost keeled over. "D'er all
crazy here. I must get back to Brooklyn. No vonder
de Yankees are t'inking about leaving de Bronx. Crazy,
It's just crazy here." As soon as the professor
returned from the bank, he drove away rapidly,
searching for any highway out of "the crazy borough"
as a throng of interested parties, bodega owners,
bank employees, and one police-humanist laughed until

the tears were streaming from their eyes.

Hamstringing the Police

Although the average police officer has tremend-
ous leverage in making decisions on the street, he
is hamstrung by borough command decisions. A hands-
off attitude on illegal social clubs where whiskey,
drugs, and guns are bought and sold is one such policy. It allows for criminal sanctuaries in every
abandoned building in which an enterprising person
has set up shop. The argument is made that the
police can not do everything - and of course they
can not - but the same activity that is crushed in
Brooklyn is permitted in the Bronx. Policemen can
go on for hours about criminal relativism - and with
good reason.

It has also been brought to my attention that
the city administration gave $70 a week to members
of the Ching-a-Lings [a youth gang] to escort elderly
women to the supermarket. That in itself is no issue,
except that this was an extortion payment to the
very same elderly, and the money is used to buy weap-
ons that are subsequently employed in a wide variety
of criminal activities, including and expecially
armed robbery. Because the Ching-a-Lings are now
engaged in a "city project," the police have been

12

told "to lay off" gang members and their headquarters in a renovated building has become as safe a criminal sanctuary as the medieval university.

When the police are not constrained by the political demands of superiors, they often face the condescension of those in interfacing institutions. The assistant district attorneys, for example, who are upper middle class, ritualistically liberal, possess an attitude of superiority which is cultivated in law school, and are embittered by the fact that they earn less than police officers, invariably have a patronizing attitude toward the police. When an arrest is made, the a.d.a. starts his interrogation with the assumption the officer has no case. "Did you inform this fellow of his constitutional rights?" "Are you sure no provocation or entrapment was demonstrated in this arrest?" There is nothing wrong with these questions and I am glad they are asked, but the tone usually suggests the officer does not know what he is doing or, at the very least, has made an error in the arrest procedure.

At one hearing in Traffic Court, the arbiter, in discussing a summons Kenny had dispensed, said, "Officer, are you sure you understand the rules of the road?" The question was dripping with condes-

cension and Kenny blew up. It was hard for me to
think of any other kind of response. After all,
he spends eight hours of every day riding a squad
car and enforcing the rules of the road. Why should
the arbiter assume Kenny did not understand traffic
laws?

These are minor irritants that, in the aggregate,
create intense stress. It is amazing that the police
generally maintain equilibrium on the job. Police
work, more often than not, has constant tension and
a lack of resolution. Jobs are not like television
productions that have a beginning, middle, and end,
with two pauses for a commercial break. Police activity is chaotic, seemingly lacking in purpose, and
yet is indispensible. The police officer cannot
make the Bronx a better place to live. He cannot
stop the arson or stem the decay. He cannot find
jobs and he cannot influence politicians. He is
often a pawn trapped between civil libertarians and
artificial production rates that measure his effect-
iveness. He is asked to put his finger in a dike
long after the flood is uncontrollable. He will
remain unappreciated and his tasks are unavoidably
Sisyphean.

My fantasies are gone. I no longer wish to

14

be a police officer. In fact, even the empty platitudes of university life seem less offensive after
this experience. However, there is a newfound and
deeper appreciation for the thankless police job.
I now have the belief that my life is a little better
for having known two fine police officers, and I
suspect that, when the elegy of the Bronx is written
and, phoenix-like, this area rises from the ashes,
some kind words will be said for those policemen
who genuinely cared when so few cared about them.

CHAPTER 2

THE COUNTER-MYTH OF POTENCY

If recent history has accomplished anything, it
is a redefinition of the future. Optimism - which
characterized a view of the American future as late
as fifteen years ago - has been replaced by fatalism.
A general cultural formulation that hard work breeds
success has retreated before the observation that
hard work is for "suckers." The American social
experiment generated optimism because - precisely
because - the future was undetermined. Americans
became inured to something William James called "the
belief in potency," a belief in man's ability to
determine his future. Whether this belief was warranted is unimportant; James realized that people
should act in accordance with it in order to secure
their freedom, independence and "the noble life."
In American history, potency was the future; it
was the prevailing value system; it was pragmatism
wrapped in faith.

One need not be a social scientist to realize
that this value system is now moribund. Bourgeois
culture, which transmitted the belief in potency,
has been undermined by the vitality of a competing
belief system described by Lionel Trilling as "adversary culture." This is not only the adversary cult of
Con III, Indian beads, gurus, and LSD, but one that
subscribes to a belief in impotence, the inability

of man to determine his future: The future is closed, or as inexorable as Marxist predictions.

Factors Underlying Impotency

To confirm the view of those espousing impotence there is the twentieth-century "science" of behaviorism. If the much abused B. F. Skinner can be cited as testimony, there exists the cast-iron effect (read control) of environment on human behavior. In his scenarios, science precludes a free choice of future. Control will be achieved by the arrangement of the environment and by the demythologizing of notions such as freedom and autonomy. Impotence enters the consciousness as the "good life." To speak of powerlessness today is chic - a little like Zen, Est, or ouija boards, which are other manifestations of the same social malaise. From boardrooms to collective bedrooms, the refrain appears to be the same: "What can you do?"

Reinforcing the conclusions of behavioristic science are three explanations of contemporary life that masquerade as truths: (1) technology is beyond our understanding and control, (2) the cold war has dissipated national will for dubious ends, and (3) most problems are subject to solution. What is interesting about these explanations is that they have

2

a momentum of their own. They are used as irrefutable claims from one end of the country to the other. But I maintain that they are quite false.

First, technology, the modern bogeyman, appears impersonal, but men and women do the programming and determine use. If technology has effects we don't like, those effects are as subject to our influence as is their cause. If the benefits of technology are not equal to the cost, they will undoubtedly be eliminated or controlled. The price of technology rises to the level of social demand. When people will pay for a given result, more often than not they will have it.

Second, the cold war does dissipate our energies, but it is hardly for dubious ends. Despite the inflated rhetoric of the last ten years, the United States has been a reluctant power, a nation obliged to fill power vacuums in order to maintain international stability. It is misleading to discuss "the arrogance of power" without reference to historical antecedents. It is worse yet to discuss foreign policy as if it is beyond our control. Post-Vietnam foreign policy may be bleak, but that is because we have made it so. By signalling chinks in our armor of resistance, we have transferred initiative to our detractors. And the less initiative we have, the more impotence intrudes on decision-making. If we are unwilling to pay the price demanded by the cold war, the most adroit diplomatic moves will not restore national potency.

And last, we have been so deluded by political promises that it is difficult to distinguish between what is possible and what we want. We are often told that if poverty is a problem, it should be solved. But how can poverty be eliminated when poverty itself is relative? If polluted streams are a problem, they should be made clean. But how can streams be clean unless personal sacrifices for cleanliness are made? If illiteracy is a problem, children should be taught to read. But why should students learn to read when an expanded definition of literacy is acceptable? We are beseiged by a utopianism that is based on the false assumption of the social cure. When the cure is not available, the prescription is either redefinition of the problem or nihilistic action. In both instances the result is the same: despair and impotence.

Yet if the errors that account for impotence are so palpable, why isn't the belief in impotence challenged? It seems to me equally obvious that

4

many have a stake in its retention. The technocrats who monopolize decision-making, because it is assumed they are endowed with special information, act to control the dissemination of data. The professional classes that reap great financial rewards will not jeopardize their status and influence by sharing competencies. Those who preach apocalypse, such as "professional revolutionaries," have also profited by telling the impotent that there is nothing else to do but revolt. Impotence, paradoxically, has vitality as long as significant portions of the population use debilitating influence for their own ends.

Resurrecting Free Will

The response to this dilemma is clear but difficult. It is the resurrection of a counter-myth of potency based on the belief that we have free will to determine our destiny. To be effective, this belief must have the transcendent qualities of a myth because it is competing with a value system rooted in well established interests. It is also a dubious notion because it requires an appreciation of nuance. But despite the difficulties, the benefits are potentially staggering. The turnaround from a culture drifting from its moorings, to one where inner strength and direction is restored, may be the only way to save the West from dissolution.

Undergirding this myth structure are several assumptions that deal with the nature of social attitudes and that ultimately determine the condition of perceived potency:

1. Free will implies the ability to affect an indeterminate future. It also presupposes that one's personal efforts can influence the course of events. If one accepts dialectical materialism as a guide to the future, one forecloses on individual potency. You cannot assume a definite goal - one which precludes all other options - and retain free will to determine the future.

2. Social policy should recognize that gran-. diose schemes cannot succeed completely. That contention, however, should not lead to hopelessness. The government may grant everyone an income of $5,000, but that cannot eliminate poverty. Moreover, the failure to eliminate poverty is not necessarily bad. With differential income rates, the incentive to improve still exists.

3. We should expect that every so-called solution generates new problems. This is in the natural order of things and should not create disillusion. If we clean the air, how does it affect the mobility

patterns that created the problem in the first place?
If we achieve "acceptable" unemployment levels, what
price will we have to pay in increased inflation?
In one theory of biology - heterosis - there is an
interesting analogue. Presumably the gene that con-
tains the potential for sickle cell anemia in a population of East Africa also provides the natural imm-
unity for malaria. Can genetic tampering avoid the
substitution of one disease for another?

    4. Individual potency within a community of
interests suggests what H.D.F. Kitto, author of
THE GREEKS, defined as arêtê, an ability to fulfill
oneself through virtuous action for the polis (city,
nation, community as a whole). One discovered "self"
through community service for the common good. Compare this idea with those of the disciples of the
human potential movement, who regard ego as everything, and "actualizing," to borrow Abraham Maslow's
term, as the life of ease, self-indulgence, and pleasure, notwithstanding the effect this behavior has
on the community.

    Metaphorically, the myth of potency characterizes
the future as a "golden age" in contradistinction
to a conceptual "brave new world." The latter model
is a social system instilled with ennui, despair,

and instant gratification. There is a loss of self as the echo for recognition reverberates. It is in effect the life of impotence. The golden age is the Periclean era revisited, with technology in harness. It is a period in which man defines himself through communal participation. It is the life of work, longing, fulfillment, and difficult decisions. It is also the life of potency.

How to get from here to there at a time when hopelessness is ubiquitous cannot be easily engineered. Undoubtedly some government action, particularly the deflation of rhetoric and the promotion of individual action for community welfare, is desirable. President Carter, in his inaugural address, has already taken steps in this direction by referring to the "new spirit among us." This is a carefully couched effort to resurrect feelings of national potency. But in the long run it is the restoration of faith that counts, faith not only in the system to restore optimism, but faith in our leaders to achieve justice and decency. With a public that is distrustful at the very least, and often cynical, and with leaders who are insecure, the essential legitimacy that supports the society has started to crumble. A slide down the path of impotence seems inevitable if we remain myopic to other options. The emergence of potency is in the avoidance of inertia; there are alternative futures if we allow ourselves to consider them.

There is a rather inspirational story of sexual impotence that demonstrates what can be done through individual will. A veteran of World War I, already in his nineties, met some of his war buddies at a recent reunion. During the course of conversation he said to his friends, "Do you remember the time when we were given saltpeter to inhibit our sexual drive?" "Sure," they responded, "but what difference does that make now?" "Well," he said, "now that I'm in my nineties, it's finally starting to take effect."

One wonders if the aphrodisiacal power of potency can restore public faith in this myth. It seems to me there is nothing to lose - we've done that already.

CHAPTER 3
AN INTERPRETATION OF FREEDOM - CIRCA 1976

The idea that "man is born free but is everywhere in chains" reflects a political belief devoid of distinctions. Freedom is related to a social context. As Freud suggested in CIVILIZATION AND ITS DISCONTENTS man is trapped by social need and personal desire. On the one hand he wishes to express himself; to be free, unencumbered by social organization and standards as guideposts for securing order and stability. Unhappily Freud concluded that men had become so sophisticated in expressing the "human instincts" of "aggression and self-destruction" that "they could now very easily exterminate one another to the last man." But while freedom of expression has its destructive capabilities, civilization has a pathology based in inhibition and guilt. Presumably without expression man is hopelessly repressed and neurotic; without the guilt there is no culture. The paradox abounds. Yet while Freud is pessimistic abouut the consequences of renunciation, it is clear, by his own admission, that without a conscience civilization reverts to the "primitive pleasure-giving experiences" of destruction.

This analysis is by no means "new" or original. It is deeply rooted in Western thought and ignored or repressed by the children of Woodstock who be-

lieved that Con III expression meant "let it all
hang out" because conscience was a social trick of
the Establishment. For Freud and his political ante-
cedent Hobbes, society depended on restraint. In
the LEVIATHAN, Hobbes unequivocally suggests that
if man is to be consistently effective in satisfying
his passions, he must learn to function within the
parameters of socially accepted behavior, that is
to say, the "public conscience" as the agency of
political law. Contrary to popular opinion this
does not necessarily circumscribe libertarian expression,it is merely a recognition of the state's right
to define the sphere within which demands on individual freedom can be made. To reject this claim is
to provide sanction for the rules of "natural combat."
Indeed the self must be harnessed, perhaps even coer-
ced. If man is to live without fear, his behavior
must be subject to rules. If man is to keep his
vanity constrained within peaceful bounds, the threat
of external force must exist. Hobbes, wisely in
my opinion, rejected the self-admonitions of morality
as a social control. Based entirely on my own obser-
vations of incorrigibles, I am convinced this point
is accurate. Fear can mediate between desire and
rectitude. It is a force that cries "Stop!" and

that can require consideration of others' needs, even at the expense of one's own.

Yet, like some primordial attribute hidden by social mores, the verities of this political analysis are continually rejected. A generation of Marcusean disciples is convinced that it must "do your own thing" unrestrained by the uptight standards of the public (read: bourgeois) conscience. In the after-glow of university riots, expression was everything. Freedom became an absolute right in the puerile minds that were sure laws only serve the advantage of the privileged class. And this I might note is not only the view of the adolescent beating on his chest for an emergent manhood. Freedom without restraint - no matter how illusory - is a goal of the larger society in the same way the elimination of poverty was a national crusade of the sixties.

A System of Restraint

In the United States the Declaration of Inde-·pendence gave an inspirational quality to the struggle for freedom, specifically defined by the Founding Fathers as political liberty. Here was the natural culmination of the Enlightenment legacy. If man is perfectible, then individual liberty is an unqual-ified good. But contrary to the view of the Jacobins, the Founders sought instrumentalities that could ensure that liberty. They sought the Hobbesian public conscience. As Montesquieu wrote, man may be born free but "no form of government is free by its nature." How then does that public conscience ensure the protection of liberty? Very simply, the answer was found in the Hobbesian predilection for restraining power with power. In a system so constituted it was believed that the free expression of a citizen or group or government could not oppress the individual. Freedom in this context was subject to the constraint of the balance, separation and countervailing influence of power.

If, as I appear to be suggesting, this argument for freedom and its limits is so compelling, why did the notion lose its vitality in the sixties? Why, indeed, did I feel like a preadolescent observing bizarre expressions of free will with horror and atavistic yearnings? There are in my opinion several philosophical explanations for the change whose combined effect has been the erosion of freedom as a legitmately constituted value.

When Jerry Rubin told the young to "Do it!" he captured the existential feeling of a generation. For many of the young and their older admirers, free expression without conventional limits was one way of assaulting "outmoded" institutions and policies "of repression." The very audacity of tearing down a university building, for example, is a symbolic way of tearing down social taboos and severing an association with bourgeois morality. It engenders the "committed spirit" the architects of the revolution deem necessary. For if so drastic a step is taken, something must be wrong. And if those in authority are unwilling to rectify the wrong, "the people" through their own free will should take authority into their hands. The deed, because it challenges normative behavior, emerges full-blown as a platitudinous ideology that at once convinces the participant of his morality, the authority's immorality and the institution's incongruity. In this climate of existential freedom one acts first and rationalizes later. With the whole complex of institutions, norms and standards as the enemy, free will poses as the savior from oppression.

Norman O. Brown characterizes this attitude best in LIFE AGAINST DEATH, when he contends that civilization and all its appurtenances must be smashed or, at least, radically changed in order to liberate primal and presumably "pure" human urges. Freedom in this context is spontaneous and momentary impulses that go beyond precedent. The limitations generated by law and morality are seen as the historical antecedents whose continuation is designed to repress free expression in the name of social order and the status quo. This sense of existentialism rejects the past as obsolete. Since sensation is not cumulative and past experiences serve to stifle free expression and pleasure, history has become the handmaiden of control. With the yesterdays expunged and the tomorrows preempted, there is nothing left but the instant whims of today. And in the minds of contemporary existentialists these whims masquerade as freedom.

Freedom in this post-Freudian analysis represents the way to unravel the Gordian knot of convention and usher in the new Golden Age. What is ignored - what apparently is always ignored - are precisely those parameters of action that give freedom its legitimacy; those social conventions that define behavior. Existentialism is an appropriate philosophy for social action when you can be assured of human responsibility, when each man considers the view of his fellow man when he acts. But is this the case? Has it ever been the case? Existentialism

6

without responsibility is arbitrary and ultimately destructive behavior. The products of the sixties who used an existential standard for their free expression invited the Watergate of repressive action. By believing freedom without restraint was the salvation from repression, freedom lost its legitimacy and encouraged further repression.

The "Feeling" of Being Free

The second philosophical explanation for freedom's erosion is the increasingly perceptual analysis of its existence. While freedom's meaning is determined by context, there are times when perceptions are so incompatible with even the minimal condition for freedom that to celebrate its existence is an exercise in doublethink. This is such a period. Young radicals and their older counterparts who have studied the catechism of popularized Marxism are infuriated by the so-called cooptation in our society that limits free expression, but are blind to the gross repression in Cuba or China or the Soviet Union. To cite these examples is evidence - these radicals would suggest - of hypocrisy or self-deception. What this biased conclusion does suggest is that notions of freedom have become less concerned with dispassionate appraisal and more involved with political

7

philosophy.

In this period, people espouse freedom when they subscribe to a prevailing social philosophy. They feel increasingly less free when that philosophy is unpersuasive. Thus laws, the Constitution and judiciaries are subordinated to feelings of satisfaction. The average working man may make his judgment about freedom on whether "the system works for him." It is futile to suggest what freedoms he actually has, how much more free he is than his counterparts in other nations or how much more freedom he possesses than his ancestors of one hundred years ago. In his view freedom is a function of social climate.

Consider, as examples, those children of the affluent middle class who are endowed by their social position with unprecedented social, economic and political freedom yet choose a life with the Reverend Moon or the Maharishi or, even more grotesquely, the Manson family where they have no options at all. Consider as well the loyalty generated in these groups and the paradoxical claim heard time and again that "for the first time I feel free." Obviously the word that is most revealing in this statement is "feel." If one is in tune with the prevailing view, even oppression can seem like freedom.

Closely related to this question of perception is the breakdown of those values that give a certain corresponding shape to the various institutions that permit free expression. When there is no consensus of values, no transcendent ideal, free will becomes the aggregation of selfish aims. A free society that is bankrupt of purpose gives birth to "free spirits" capable of any action, especially the most irrational. As Irving Kristol has noted, "under the strain of modern life, whole classes of the popu- lation...are entering what can only be called, in the strictly clinical sense, a phase of infantile regression." Freedom in this society - with its purpose more vague than ever before - translates into a population that is ungovernable. With liber- tarianism united with solipsism the operating prin- ciple is "I can do what you can't." The principles of sensible restraint that once organized public life appear to have little relation to private lives, a condition that escalates the degree of estrangement and vitiates the role of established authority.

Legitimate Inequality

A legitimate society, according to Aristotle, is one in which inequalities of property or status or power are generally perceived as necessary for the common good. Notwithstanding the contentiousness in this view, it was the undergirding assumption in this system. Moreover it is the feature of inequality - with modifications in the extreme - that gave vitality to the idea of freedom. For if men are unique and if they do have free will, there will naturally emerge inequality of result. Unless one accepts the assumption that all men are created exactly equal, freedom necessarily leads to inequality. This conception was accepted as long as inequality was believed to serve the common good. But once this conception was called into question, so too was the attendant value of freedom.

In the sixties - due in no small part to the work of Christopher Jencks and John Rawls - an egalitarian ideal, once the dream of Utopian Socialists, reached a conscious and active stage. What this ideal attacked was the notion of equality of opportunity and substituted for it a belief in the equality of result - a belief that insisted on relatively equal wages and status regardless of position. Whether this position has merit - a view I seriously doubt - is not the subject of this article. What this egalitarian stance implies is, however, of major importance. For if incomes are to be distributed equally; if status is to be parcelled out like food stamps, who is responsible for the distribution and on what basis? One concomitant of this system - one that logically and empirically follows - is that free will must be controlled. The desire for rewards from demonstrated individual talent must be curbed. Freedom, in other words, must move aside for orchestrated equality.

As these views gained adherents there was a two-fold and curiously overlapping effect: Freedom became an obstacle to be opposed and overcome and freedom as an extreme - "do your own thing," "polymorphous perversity" - was embraced as a strategy for social change. What revolutionaries of the sixties desired was the use of free choice inherent in bourgeois society as a way to destroy that very same society for the "higher ideal" of the egalitarian ethic. As a consequence of this contradictory posturing, the average man, who has faith in freedom as a consensual value, gradually observed the selective interpretation of the value and the unravelling of the consensus. The free society became less free as the constraints that determined freedom could not be determined.

Freedom is not a myth to be debunked like George Washington and the cherry tree; it is a partial truth. It exists only within limits; consequently it cannot be undiluted. To be free is to know limits, just as knowing pleasure is dependent on pain. Similarly, freedom depends on a past. Historical antecedents give the notion consensual acceptance. To be free for an existentialist suggests that restraint is self-imposed and subject only to self-rejection. Freedom is a corollary of the social system. Believing oneself free is a prerequisite, albeit rarely the result, of being free. And freedom within a social system is incompatible with equality. If one can express himself, inequality is the likely result.

In consideration of this idea of freedom and its rationale, B.F Skinner in BEYOND FREEDOM AND DIGNITY contends that there isn't an "autonomous man," an absolutely free individual. If my analysis has any validity, he is probably right. Where he is wrong, however, is in suggesting that the "traditional idea" of freedom that relied on inalienable liberties is part of an historical pattern. Environmental conditions established a consensual view of freedom throughout history. When there were no rewards or a consensus that could sustain the idea,

12

freedom was curbed. What emerges from Skinner's work, especially <u>WALDEN II</u>, is not a defense of a "new freedom" or even a strategy for its continuation, but rather a view that whether freedom is attainable or not is inconsequential. In choosing the "good life" or the "free life" - assuming they are mutually exclusive - Skinner comes down hard for the former. For a generation conditioned by Skinnerian truths it is little wonder that freedom has lost her loveliness. A technology of behavior has seemingly made freedom the culprit of our social woe. And <u>BRAVE NEW WORLD</u> enters our consciousness as the "good life."

CHAPTER 4

TODAY'S GRAY-LISTING OF THE RIGHT

An ad for a current film, "The Front," reads, "In 1953 this film could not have been made." In 1976 that film has been made, but others, of a different political persuasion, can't be. The blacklist which haunted writers with pinkish complexions has been replaced with a blacklist for anti-Communists. Media hypes ignore the latest political litmus test, which rejects writers if they aren't at least somewhat pinkish.

If this sounds like the angry voice of an unpublished author, it is only partially true. My work is published, although not as often as I'd like. And the reason for rejection is very bluntly stated as "my ideas." It would be different if my writing skill were challenged or if that were used as a rationalization, but invariably the comment is the same: "You write well and with humor but your ideas are too conservative for this house." Now what the hell is too conservative? I do believe Hayek contributed more to economics than Galbraith; I consider Solzhenitsyn the only genuine hero in the world; I think Reagan's posture on welfare in California was progressive and I maintain that Bella Abzug has the instincts of a Stalinist. These are obviously not my only views but these are the ones that virtually assure rejection.

"How can you make claims about so few conservatives represented in the media?" I'm often asked.
Bill Buckley appears on prime-time television shows.
Ernest Van den Haag's boon on crime and punishment
made the best-seller lists. And Irving Kristol's
words of wisdom can be found in The Wall Street Journal. Yet these examples of conservative celebrities
are trotted out like token blacks at AT&T affirmative action meetings. Their opinions have about
as much influence with media panjandrums as profes-
sorial arguments at Chamber of Commerce meetings.
One executive editor said, "Last year we even published two books by conservatives."

It is instructive - I believe - to consider
the lesson in the following dialogue between a pro-
spective agent and yours truly. "I like your work,
Prof. London," she noted hesitantly. "You certainly
don't write like an academic. But I won't accept
any clients whose work I don't believe in. And
I can't support your views." Now I don't need an agent
who supports my views; only one who can sell them.
Once again I am subjected to the political screening
test. I sometimes want to lie; to play the game
of committing myself to the general well-being of

every conceivable underdog. But I can't do it. I
am so steeped in preserving an independent position
that the lures of success - at least so far - have
not accounted for a change in my attitudes.

Of course there is the strategy of adopting
conservative views and calling them liberal. This
technique, refined by politicians like Gov. Brown
of California, might very well have an application
in publishing. The question, of course, is whether
authors are permitted the same degree of misrepresen-
tation as politicians. I think not, but then again
there are examples of liberals like John Kenneth
Galbraith who discover that they are really socialists
after all and don't mind the new designation.

With pencils ready to defend the bastions of
the liberal establishment, editors draw lines across
the pages of conservative works as symbols of their
victory. Professors of journalism encourage their
students to be Woodward and Bernstein, not Walter
Lippman. Book review editors use a political standard
for authors who aren't well known. The works of
a Buckley or a Muggeridge can't be rejected for fear
that charges of egregious bias will be made; but
the books of lesser conservative lights qualify only
for anonymity. I could be mistaken, but my experience

3

suggests that in the world of publishing, being right
is wrong and being left is right.

CHAPTER 5
ATTITUDES TOWARD POVERTY

A report on poverty in New York City one hundred years ago indicated, "The streets of New York became thronged with this ragged, starving crowd; they filled all the stationhouses and lodging-places provided by private charity and overflowed into the island almshouses." This description conjures an image very different from the demands of contemporary welfare rights groups for a guaranteed annual wage of $5,000 for a family of four.

Policies of any kind are usually based on prevailing attitudes. Nutritional needs, for example, are related to the demands of occupation and leisure time. They may also be a function of expectations: though steer liver is more nutritionally desirable and less expensive than filet mignon, the filet is usually preferred. A comprehensive nutritional policy based on eating preferences would inferentially suggest that the poor have an equal opportunity for arteriosclerosis. Health needs are influenced by longevity; education needs by personal goals; and self-actualization - to use Maslow's over-used phrase - by surplus income.

Poverty and policies affecting poverty are inextricably woven into the fabric of historical development. It is obviously inappropriate to discuss the poverty of one locale without relating it to the social evolution of a nation. In examining attitudes toward poverty, therefore, one must actually examine the social context in which poverty exists. Even then, what must be considered are those cataclysmic events such as war, prosperity, and inflation that give poverty definition and those legislative poli= cies that create a "poverty level" for political pur- poses or reflect prevailing popular attitudes toward the subject.

Origin of Aid to the Poor

The English experience with poverty quite natur- ally had an influence, albeit not always a direct one, on American attitudes toward the poor. Despite the widespread poverty in the sixteenth century, the main burden of support rested with benevolent citizens. There was a dramatic acceptance of social responsibility by an extraordinary number of private citizens, many of whom were affluent and others of only moderate means. Tudor legislation on poverty, notably the Poor Laws of 1597 - 1601, was to be in- voked only if the situation exceeded the capacity of private philanthropy. It was through this charity that an ethic of social responsibility emerged, an ethic that was ultimately to be the hallmark of

2

liberal society.

The tradition of social responsibility was reinforced by the compulsions of Calvinist doctrines.
In particular, the stress on the stewardship of one's
wealth had much to do with developing habits of philanthropy. This spirit coincided with the economic
revolution and population explosion in England and
the attendant growth of cities, surplus labor, and
a strained social structure. Conditions were generally so bad from the sixteenth to the nineteenth
centuries that many accepted a surplus labor force
as immutable. Indeed, since Englishmen were increasing at the rate of 14 percent per decade after the
eighteenth century, there was prima facie evidence
to support that conclusion. Most middle- and upper-
class Englishmen accepted "the poor" as a given,
a permanent element of the social structure from
which only a few could rise in each generation. It
was argued in word and deed that the vast majority
must make their own terms with the inevitable and carry
their burdens without depending on others. To assist
the poor unduly was simply "to pauperize," to make
public charges of those quite capable of caring for
themselves.

3

Transplantation in the New World

As historian R.H. Bremner, author of FROM THE
DEPTHS and other significant works on poverty,
suggests, "The tradition of philanthropic service
was easily transplanted in the New World." There
were signs of it in Cotton Mather's claim that
Boston's aid to the poor was "well and favorably
known in Heaven." However, without the feudal posture of noblesse oblige, philanthropy was treated with
suspicion. Americans expect the wealthy to contribute to good causes; then we question their motives
or deplore the way their wealth was acquired. Or
we wonder if the gift does more harm than good. The
givers may be labeled "bleeding hearts" and "senti-
mentalists"; their contributions may be described
as patronizing to the less fortunate; yet we recognize the institutions their money has built as major
social advances.

Since this country was founded on a scarcity
of labor, as opposed to the English labor surplus,
it was accepted from the outset that it was unneces-
sary for the able-bodied poor to be economically dependent. Where poverty existed, it was a function
of varying ability and incentive to work. In both
cause and cure, the fate of poverty was up to the

4

individual. Poverty could be a goad to success or
a penalty for failure to compete; it could be the
incentive for Horatio Alger or the breeding ground
for Al Capone.

For the Puritans, self-help in economic matters
was closely related to the spirit of religion. Salvation through personal regeneration was based on
the idea that heaven was open to those who proved
themselves worthy, just as financial success was
possible for those who had faith in free enterprise.
"Good works don't make a good man, but a good man
makes good works." All that is necessary in this
system is the freedom to demonstrate one's goodness,
if this goodness was predestined by God. An ethic
of individual responsibility provided the psychological attitude, personal discipline, and rationale
for a faith in advancement. Poverty, when it existed,
was not ignored; but it was considered a providential
decree of a person's weakness. Its cure, therefore,
was a heightened sense of personal responsibility;
and when that was not possible, as in the case of
the infirm, individuals would be assigned to care
for those unable to care for themselves.

Up to the eighteenth century, the basic conception of philanthropy was that almsgiving was not

designed to assist those in need of help but was
a means of demonstrating the donor's goodness and
virtue in the eyes of God. However, a competing
faith in the Enlightenment tradition and its inspirational view of independence generated a belief
in the perfectibility of man. From this stance,
the person requiring aid was the challenge, and assistance to the needy was not so much charity as a
means by which society acted to improve itself. Uni-
versalists and Unitarians in the nineteenth century,
proclaiming neither earthly want nor predestined damna-
tion, argued that man could purify himself of the
"bad habits" that led to indigence. This might be
achieved by a "personal determination to avoid evil"
and a move toward the path of morality and self-
discipline. Although the theoretical cause of poverty differed for Puritans and Unitarians, the cure -
personal discipline and responsibility - was one
and the same.

Darwin and His Critics: A 19th-Century Dilemma

While the eighteenth and much of the nineteenth
centuries relied on rational and transcendental religious thought to justify the ideal of the "independent man," it took the Darwinians to assert this ideal
as a scientific axiom. According to Herbert Spencer

and his disciples, protecting the poor in their struggle for survival was tantamount to weakening the species. Darwinism had invested the previous ideal of self-reliance with an even greater purity. Further, an article of faith had it that this nation was sufficiently open so that the common man could become the self-made man. With barriers to equal opportunity eliminated, only personal weakness could explain failure. Therefore, no rights were accorded the poor. Relief was still a Christian duty, but it was an act at the discretion of the donor, not an act demanded by the recipient's condition.

Darwinism combined with the shibboleths of the Gilded Age to make laissez-faire and self-reliance fundamental laws of nature and of God. But there were critics of the notion and competing attitudes born of conditions and tradition. However much the creed of self-help reigned, there was the derivative Christian ideal of communal assistance for the down-trodden. Many Protestants contended that their Christian obligation compelled them to make the church and gospel relevant for the underprivileged. Others believed in the possibilities of redeeming the poor.

By the late nineteenth century, it was apparent that charity reform conflicted with the spirit of individualism. This was the essential paradox in the national mood: a desire for the elimination of poverty was incompatible with the self-reliance demanded of industrialization. Similarly, with the depression in the 1870s and the 1890s, critics claimed that no laborer was as free as formerly to determine how or whether his work would be rewarded. As class lines became more rigid than they were before the Civil War, and as hard-working men joined the ranks of the poor, a demand for relief from the assumed natural laws of laissez-faire gained support. The growth of private insurance plans, settlement houses, and state relief agencies in the 1880s reflected a public desire to hedge its bets on self-reliance.

Charity Reformers

There emerged from the general dissatisfaction with laissez-faire an ideological view that scorned competition as unethical and irresponsible. Christian Socialists in the beginning of the twentieth century viewed poverty as a problem capable of solution if only "unwholesome individualism" and its attendant laissez-faire philosophy could be controlled. They argued that the "invisible hand" of individual enterprise and the consequent concern for self-interest

could not serve to bind men together for mutual benefit. Their conception of poverty was translated
into charity organizations that attempted to redeem
the poor and eliminate street begging and vagrancy.
The Christian Socialists, the most notable of the
charity reformers of their time, became increasingly
preoccupied with the obvious distinction between
poverty, which unavoidable, and pauperism, which
was deemed avoidable and wasteful. It was the latter
notion that concerned them because, presumably, pauperism was capable of solution. The "work test,"
the test of "a man's willingness to be a man," the
test that distinguished the worthy from the unworthy,
was the litmus paper for poverty at the turn of the
nineteenth century. But the Christian Socialists
maintained that the work test ignored indifference
and selfishness parading under the banner of inevitable economic cycles.

For these reformers, the poor were victims of
social disintegration. As "helpless pawns of industry", the poor were not only without money, they were
lonely, isolated, and friendless. While the mid-
nineteenth-century charity gave "bread and coal,"
the reform voices of the twentieth century argued
for a "hand, heart, and brain." When William Graham

Sumner, the ultimate Darwinist, said, "What can one social class demand of another? Nothing can be demanded," the reformers retorted, "Goodness, morality, and religion impose obligations." The reformers rejected Sumner because they viewed a society not as each against all but as an organic entity in which the misfortunes of one affected the fortunes of all.

The utopianism of the reformers was not always in harmony with the complex reasons for poverty, such as upbringing, peer-group attitudes, expectations, disappointments, unemployment both avoidable and unavoidable. The charity reformers assumed that individual moral weakness caused shiftlessness and degradation; yet despite "scientific investigations" by social scientists eager to determine causation, this was not easily proved. Similarly, the Christian Socialists claimed that the vicissitudes of the economic cycle led to unsatisfactory rewards for even the hard-working employee at times of prosperity. But no one could determine what unsatisfactory rewards were. What is physical efficiency or those goods and services necessary for a "decent" standard of living?

Progressivism and the New Deal

In 1892, Henry Adams presaged the Progressive

spirit by asking: "Who does not know that much of
our so-called philanthropy tends to blunt the edge
of our moral perception and, consequently, to perpet-
uate those conditions which seem to make philanthropy
necessary?" At a time when it was widely accepted
that a private welfare system gave more honor to
the donor and less damage to the recipient, Adams
meant to acknowledge the social apathy toward poverty
that resulted from a reliance on private assistance.
As long as private charity seemingly had the primary
obligation for custodial care of the poor, it appeared as if little more need be done.

With the rise of Progressivism, a struggle was
launched to abolish the poverty that an earlier generation believed could not, under any circumstances,
be eradicated. The assumption of many Progressives
in the twentieth century - by no means all of them -
was that poverty could be attacked through government
programs. The strain of late-nineteenth-century
depressions created the idea that relief should be
provided as a right and not as a privilege. Although
it took three decades for the idea to germinate and
emerge full-blown, it was clear that the attitudes
of the Progressive Era had successfully challenged
laissez-faire assumptions and insistence on self-

reliance. This is not to suggest that self-reliance was rejected. At first, it coexisted with the welfare ideal as a mutually compatible notion along with the argument that public assistance and welfare reform were temporary devices that allowed an individual to cope while seeking employment or planning to strike out on his own.

The Progressives, while taking a dim view of sentimental charity, were trying to reinvigorate social responsibility without weakening individual responsibility. But economic conditions made government intrusion irresistible. In fact, the economic cycle seemed to present incontrovertible evidence that private charity could not cope with the problems of modern society. Events during the Great Depression ultimately demonstrated the need for at least some government involvement in the matter of assistance for the downtrodden.

From the New Deal emerged the view that unemployment would have to be considered as more than a casual, peripheral enterprise. It was obvious that emergency measures advocated by an earlier generation of reformers were insufficient to meet a problem of national proportions. At first the New Dealers relied on precedents of the past, such as municipal adminis-

tration for assistance, but the scope of the financial
emergency made active federal involvement in the
support of the poor irresistible.

Mid-20th-Century Assumptions

By mid-century it could be maintained that the
challengers to pre-Progressive Era notions about
poverty had established a conventional wisdom based
on government assistance. This rationale included
the folowing characteristics:

1. Aid to the dependent poor is their right,
   not a privilege;

2. Dependency not only involves the absence
   of "sufficient funds" but "psychological
   deprivation," a deprivation cited by Christian Socialists as a key factor in the re-
   curring condition of family poverty;

3. The society should assume responsibility
   for poverty, not the poor themselves;

4. Legal service, which has its origins in
   the Legal Aid developed by the German Immigrant Society in the 1880s, should be provided for all the poor in order to prevent
   state elimination of their right to assistance.

5. Aid does not suppose only welfare or sub-

13

sistence but also sufficient funds and services to provide a "decent" standard of living, a standard institutionalized by social science research during and after the New Deal.

What these assumptions suggest is that sometime between the New Deal period and the mid 1960s, the reluctant but irreversible direction of further federal government involvement in poverty matters became an active and affirmative commitment to eliminate the presence of poverty. The Progressive spirit manifested as moral concern became a political solution.

With the violence and national soul-searching that characterized the urban riots of the sixties came a challenge to the classic liberal assumption that continuous expansion of the Gross National Product at the 4 or 5 percent per year rate would ultimately lead to the elimination of poverty. It was obvious that the expansion of the GNP did not affect entrenched pockets of poverty that were resistant to the general expansion of national wealth. Liberals were forced to choose - this is what polarization was all about - between a respect for law that overlooked the appalling conditions of poverty and a

14

demonstration of immediate concern for the poor that overlooked law, precedents, and previous policy. The decision to opt for a War on Poverty revealed which direction the Democrat-dominated government took.

Whether one accepts the argument made by Frances Fox Piven and Richard Cloward that poverty policies were directly related to political realignments in the inner-city or Gilbert Steiner's view that administrative neglect and ignorance of the consequences created an atmosphere whereby temporary, makeshift programs became permanent, the fact remains that politics in the decade of the sixties dictated a set of poverty reforms. These reforms were reinforced by institutions organized to eliminate "the poverty problem." For example, legal services successfully challenged state efforts to limit welfare eligibility; government agencies organized the poor to picket welfare departments as part of a legitimate strategy for further assistance; the Office of Economic Opportunity contended that participation of the poor in policy making was necessary to overcome the psychological deprivation of powerlessness brought on by their impoverished state; and welfare rights groups were organized to demand increased assistance to dependent people. In most respects, the tentative character of early-twentieth-century reforms became entrenched policies and the rationale for government assistance dictated practice.

Entitlements

The sensitizing of a generally affluent population to the conditions of poverty - through such works as Michael Harrington's OTHER AMERICA - created a climate of concern where entitlements were made possible. It became commonplace in the late sixties and early seventies to observe welfare recipients who own color television sets organize and picket for a guaranteed income. They were joined in the "struggle" for entitlements by guilt-ridden liberals, unreconstructed New Dealers, and idealists of various persuasions who sought an identification with the downtrodden for what Edward Banfield described as a need for "psychic satisfaction." There were, of course, the needy desperate for assistance and the social reformers with genuine motives for their involvement, but with the overheated rhetoric of the period, it was difficult to make distinctions.

In short order, wants replaced needs - to use Aristotelian terms - and "wants by their nature are unlimited and unsatiable." Since attitudes toward consumption had been freed from the constraints of the Protestant Ethic in the affluent post-war era, and since many of the affluent believed there was enough to go around for everyone, accumulation of goods and a right to possess them became inalienable. Even with a major recession upon us, the expectation of a job and a rising standard of living, and, consequently, entitlements, remains undiminished. There has been no real distinction between "absolute" and "relative" poverty since the mid-twentieth century, in spite of jargon that insists on a "poverty level." Now it is firmly established that poverty can be regarded only as relative deprivation.

Where poverty of the nineteenth century was viewed as inevitable, a part of the ebb and flow of history, it is now considered an aberration of the times that can be eliminated with Keynesian formulas. This attitude is perpetuated by administrations that can reject the notion only with severe risk to their survival. How can a government that wins public support with its intention of creating needed social programs suggest that the need is not greater than the financial risk in operating the programs? The answer is that it must go into debt or call into question its legitimacy.

More Aid, More Poverty

What emerges from this brief survey of attitudes toward poverty and welfare proposals is the evolution of an idea. For much of American history, poverty was regarded as either a natural condition influenced by providence or a function of character flaws. In either event, social assistance, while always existing, was limited to those cases where no other means of support was available. What society demanded was contrition from the poor and a well-developed sense of self-help from the general population. The strain in this belief came with extended depressions in which some employables, eager to work, could not find jobs. As a consequence, personal responsibility gave way to social responsibility. Aid evolved from a privilege to a practice to a right to an entitlement. George Homans perspicaciously explained this point when he noted: "The more often... an activity emitted under particular stimulus conditions has been rewarded, the more anger will be displayed...when the same activity emitted under similar conditions goes without its reward. Precedents are always turning into rights."

The change in attitude toward poverty resulted in both a quantitative as well as a qualitative

change in what it meant to be poor. During the sixties - a period of relative affluence despite spiral-
ing inflation - the welfare rolls escalated dramatically in every major city. Conditions could not
be described as worse than the previous decade, but
our perception of them had changed. Poverty was
simply not acceptable, not for the most affluent
nation in the world, a nation that had, moreover,
marshaled its resources for a war against it.

Just as public assistance moved from a privilege
to a right, poverty itself changed from a condition
of unfortunate circumstances that required temporary
relief to a situation that warranted affection,
friendship, psychological treatment, and massive
public concern. Social work was more than processing
names on relief rolls; it was a public service that
required an analysis of the symptoms of "social pathology," which led to the conclusion, more often than
not, that the poor are the flotsam and jetsam of
industrialization, "pawns of capitalism."

That the attendant problems of poverty - like
crime and apathy - remained even when the poor had
more money was one of those social facts that was
conspicuously ignored by those with a vested interest
in the maintenance of assistance programs. The

irresistible force of a bureaucracy with a stake
in assisting the poor perpetuates the idea of "poverty
levels." And a well-developed sense of social responsibility on the part of many of the affluent, a faith
in entitlements, and the cynicism of government officials eager to maintain political support contribute
to the notion that poverty can be eliminated.

Meanwhile, conditions do improve - even if there
is disagreement on how much. But as the relative
difference in income declines, especially between
the working-poor and welfare-poor, the class differ-
ences that remain are exaggerated. To illustrate:
between 1936 and 1950 the income of the highest quintile of all income recipients rose by 32 percent,
and the income of the lowest quintile by 125 percent.
Furthermore, from 1956 to 1967 median white income
rose 46.6 percent while median black income rose
76.2 percent. "By 1970 there remained no difference
between young (under 35) husband-and-wife families,
white or black." Yet the trend toward equalization
that pervaded the entire structure did not create
widespread satisfaction. It is axiomatic that there
is little competition for status between the person
who earns $10,000 and the one who earns $50,000 a
year; while there is likely to be more envy when one

earns $10,000 and another earns $12,000 for similar work.

It may very well be that the egalitarian surge of the past two decades cannot be resisted. Some form of guaranteed income establishing greater equality than the present tax system is likely - which accounts in no small part for the growing popularity of the negative income tax. But the paradox in providing further aid to the poor is that more aid creates more "poverty". Attitudes toward poverty have conspired to create a situation where the more aid we have the worse it gets. With more aid and more social workers than ever before, and a heightened sense of social responsibility, the welfare rolls grow and the poor are increasingly disenchanted.

If a female-headed family of three in New York City obtains an income - including welfare payments, medical assistance, clothing allowance, rent subsidies, food stamps - of $11,500 and the average family income in the city is $10,500, a disincentive to work and an incentive to go on welfare clearly exists. Empirically, entitlements work where everyone enjoys equal benefits for relatively equal output. But that is not the prevailing attitude. Wants appear to have outstripped gives by a substantial margin. And if anything is true, it appears that more people

21

want more for less than was ever the case. Even
if the unlikely egalitarian utopia suggested by John
Rawls were upon us, equality could exist only when
expectations are curbed, when people will produce
more and accept less.

Our present attitudes have already become an
indulgence we can ill afford. In New York City,
for example, from 1960 to 1973 the number of persons
on welfare tripled while the rate of unemployment
was halved and poverty decreased. In the same period
there was a notorious shortage of unskilled labor.
Yet jobs remained unfilled because the price of poverty was higher or comparable to the price of labor.
As long as the system suggests that it pays to be
poor, the government can expect the poverty level
to rise to the price being offered. Moreover, as
long as the government depends for its support on
various forms of public assistance, the national
debt will increase, and those living at the margin
or on a fixed income will be driven to despair. For
the long run, it does not require a sophisticated
imagination to conceive of a scenario of rebellion
and conflict over the issue of who works and who
doesn't, and who pays the taxes for those who receive
the assistance. In consideration of conditions like

these, Pitirim Sorokin noted, societies rise and fall on their attitudes toward poverty, equality, and privilege.

A REHABILITATION PROGRAM THAT WORKS

From the pen of social scientists comes the same dismal conclusion about criminals: there is no rehabilitation program that works. Recidivism of enormous proportions characterizes the history of American prisoners.

Drug addicts invariably return to drugs; rapists to rape and felons to new and even more reprehensible felonies. For years I have been convinced that despite the infusion of tax dollars into the prison system this pattern would remain unaltered. Now, however, I am not sure my view is accurate; to my surprise I've discovered a rehabilitation program that not only works, but is practically foolproof.

No one ever called this place a rehabilitation center and, interestingly, felons go there voluntarily. But without question it is the most effective rehabilitation agency on earth.

A stay there does to social pathology what penicillin does to infection. And the effect of being there isn't debilitating as is the case with imprisonment on the Russian steppe.

Where is the mecca of social experimentation? It is the land of tyrants and radicals in North Africa: Algeria.

This is not exactly a land of enlightened values.

Civil liberty has about as much influence on politics
as my cynical opinions on Russian military policy.
Algerian leaders proclaim an identification with
Third World extremists, which accounts in part, for
the gravitation of ingenuous radicals to this land
of perceived Marxist hospitality.

But the only actual evidence of hospitality is
the free offering of enough radical reading material
to bore recipients into conversion to different politics or the wish for imprisonment.

Eldridge Cleaver, who defended rape as a revolutionary act and who was engaged in a shootout with
police in 1968, packed his bags and sought asylum
in Algeria rather than face a San Quentin prison.

After almost two years in Algeria his belief
in a radical utopia was transformed into Christian
rectitude. This self-confessed rapist and robber
is now among our nation's leading spokesmen for the
teachings of Jesus. A short sentence in Algeria
did what San Quentin could only promise.

Similarly, the guru of L.S.D., Timothy Leary,
fearful of a long prison term for the possession
of drugs, also sought refuge in Algeria. Leary discovered what every foreign radical already knew,
drugs aren't compatible with Marxist ideology.

2

So after an imposed cold turkey, Leary decided
an American courtroom was more desirable than the
sands of North Africa. In short order, he was back
home writing for the National Review about the virtues
of the American system.

Yes, that's the same National Review of Buckley
and Rusher; a journal that should not be confused with
the New York Review, where one would expect to read
Leary's words of wisdom.

Leary discovered that there are rewards for apost-
asy that Algerians simply cannot fathom. By experi-
encing Algeria anything became acceptable, even the
formerly repressive, "fascist" land whose laws he
couldn't accept.

These examples, and hundreds of unheralded ones,
suggest a new direction for foreign aid and, as a
corollary, for policy toward criminal rehabilitation.

Stated bluntly, foreign aid to Algeria should
be considered if that government will consider the
acceptance of American criminals, particularly those
whose actions are politically inspired.

The rate of assistance will be determined by
the rate of reformed criminals who can't wait to
return to the United States.

From the Algerian standpoint this has an obvious

3

financial advantage as well as the propagandistic value of appearing to be a haven for "political criminals" who are oppressed in the United States.

If the past is any guide, the Algerians can't lose. Since anyone who spends some time there is likely to find America congenial, rehabilitation is simply a function of visiting. All the Algerians have to do to cash in is to permit unrestricted immigration.

Rarely does the possibility of a mutually beneficial policy with a rival become so apparent as is the case in this proposal. Algeria needs our money and we need her rehabilitative skills.

The peripheral consequences are equally enticing. With closer ties between the two states, Algeria might take the lead in promoting peace in the Middle East; the American crime rate might actually decrease and Algerians would bless us because they would not have to read impenetrable Marxist literature that would be reserved for American emigres.

Who ever said rehabilitation doesn't work? With this plan we might have reformed criminals, new allies and peace at home.

CHAPTER 7
WHERE ARE THE MORALISTS?

The year was 1968. The war in Vietnam entered our bedrooms as millions watched napalm bombs scorch the earth in a land far away. There were 150,000 American solders fighting in the jungles of Indochina. And from Cambridge to Berkeley there were candlelight vigils protesting the war.

Self-proclaimed moralists said it was the wrong war and were in it for the wrong reasons. George McGovern noted that when Communists take over a village "they don't assassinate people there. They set up a school and a road system and a tax system." Then why were we there?

The domino theory was categorically dismissed by many students. The protection of rights for citizens in an authoritarian South Vietnam seemed absurd. And the desire to protect the South Vietnamese from their liberators to the north seemed like taking the side of King George against George Washington. After all, I was told by students and colleagues, any comparison between an authoritarian and a totalitarian regime is a nuance without a difference. Besides, it was alleged, communism is what those people want.

It was senseless to point out that elections only took place in the south so that what Vietnamese

wanted was not easy to determine. The moralists
were sure the elections were rigged anyway. Logic
prevailed only in the Catch-22 symbolism of the dem-
onstrators.

I suggested to my detractors that a bloodbath
would make the Mekong turn crimson with the departure
of American troops. But this argument was discarded
with all my others as alarmist trash, a figment of
my anti-alarmist trash, a figment of my anti-Communist
paranoia. What could possibly be worse than what
American solders were doing to the Vietnamese?

Ten years later is probably too soon for revi-
sionist history, but the record is now coming into
focus. If the domino theory is fiction then why
does the red flag fly in the capitals of South Vietnam, Laos and Cambodia? If visions of a "bloodbath"
were apocryphal how does one explain the slaughter
in Cambodia?

As Carl Gershman points out: "Even writers
once sympathetic to Khmer Rouge, like Jean Lacouture
and Le Monde's Patrice de Beer, have described the
Cambodian upheaval as the bloodiest and most extreme
revolution in history. It represents, at the very
least, the worst crime to have been committed by
a government against a people since Hitler's destruc-

tion of the Jews.

Yet where are the moralists now? We watch in
fear and anger as television recreates the monstrous
horror of Auschwitz. We are told to remember and
remember we should. But what do we say and do about
the mass slaughter in South Vietnam and Cambodia?

Our morality has been contaminated by the
scourge of relative standards. We accept only what
is not too painful. There is, unfortunately, nothing
we can now do about Auschwitz, even if it has seared
a part of our collective memory. But we can speak
out against the genocide in Indochina.

Our conscience - to the extent that the Vietnam debacle has left us with any - demands it. Even
though protesters focused on an opposition to American involvement in Vietnam, the nature of their
protests implied the endorsement of a general moral
principle against indiscriminate killing.

Yet where are Ramsey Clark, Mary McCarthy,
Eugene McCarthy, George McGovern, Noam Chomsky, the
Berrigans, the Chicago Seven, Anthony Lewis, Allard
Lowenstein, Jane Fonda, Vanessa Redgrave now? Who
is marching for peace? Where is the voice of the
bleeding heart crying out for human decency? What
has the Pope said about the latest act of genocide?

3

J'accuse. I accuse you of hypocrisy, of deceit, of moral relativism. I accuse you of complacency in the face of horrors comparable to the last holocaust.

Many times in the last 20 years I have heard and even said, "Never again!" But "never again" is here, in the mass grave now called Democratic Kampuchea (formerly Cambodia), with the self-immolation of 12 Buddhist nuns and priests in 1975 to protest against Communist repression (Can you recall the international bravura when one Buddhist priest killed himself in 1963 as a protest against the Diem regime?) and with the thousands fleeing by foot and dinghy to be stopped at the borders of freedom and forced to return to their funerals.

Where is our conscience now? It is worn like a talisman to protect us from the horror of our own actions.

We have recoiled from the Vietnam involvement and,ostrich-like,regard only our fate as the sole source of concern. When that happens the moralists will lead us in a new crusade. One discovers at such moments that the attempt to reject an idea often becomes a novel way of being captured by it. It was Nietzche who put this message in its most unfor-

gettable form: "Beware lest a statue slay you."
That may have already happened.

CHAPTER 8
IT'S TAX REVOLT TIME AGAIN

In years to come, the vote on Proposition 13 in California will be known as the beginning of The Great Tax Revolt. The message is clear: the average citizen will not tolerate excessive government expenditures. If Gov. Brown embraces the idea that "small is beautiful," then he is going to have to live with a smaller and hopefully more beautiful budget.

Seemingly, Americans have awakened to the monstrous lie that government programs are designed to assist the poor. In reality what has been happening is that the productive middle-income groups (those earning between $15,000 and $40,000) are being taxed at King John rates to support many nonproductive and even more anti-productive bureaucrats in the same income range.

In many respects this California assault on government spending is reminiscent of conditions in New York City in the early 1840s. New York Citizen editorials of that day were calls to the barricades: "We have commenced a war against high taxes and extravagant government." Charges of exorbitant taxes, government inefficiency and profligacy were so widespread that the Nativist Party, unable to influence voters significantly in the 1820s and '30s, elected a New York mayor in 1844.

Interestingly, Samuel F. B. Morse, inventor of the telegraph, running for mayor of New York City as the Nativist Party candidate in the early 1830s, was in a hopeless minority. Although his party was a precursor to the Know-Nothing Movement (so called because its adherents were notoriously close-mouthed about their politics) of the 1850s, it is important to note that, despite the party's anti-Catholic and anti-immigrant posture, it was unable to achieve widespread voting success until it combined nativism with tax reduction.

This reform movement - as it was then described - was designed to castigate the selfish and corrupt practices of the Democratic and, to some extent, Whig officials who pandered to recently arrived immigrants. Their efforts were focused primarily on that government spending which allegedly was employed as bribes and favors in order to sway the votes of undecided newcomers.

Who can deny the similarity in motives today? Government positions are so often either patronage plums or a way of affecting group voting patterns. A balanced ticket is a euphemism for ethnic representation in government. One could argue that our problem is not big government but bad government,

2

government that has lost sight of its original mission to protect life, liberty and property, and provide for national defense.

Predictably, those who opposed Proposition 13 tended to be either the very wealthy, or the recipients of government largesse. The very rich, who like the advantages of tax-exempt bonds, will find that with the reduced state revenue their investments will, in most cases, depreciate in value. And officials, Civil Service employees and those who have been on the public dole, will find the government is no longer the easiest institution from which to secure a fast buck. The old chestnut that "if you don't want to work, take a job with the government," may have a distinctly hollow ring in the years to come.

A specter is sweeping the country. It is not the specter of socialist influence, nor it is the continual expression of government encroachment in our lives to which we have become inured. It is an old voice and a new voice. It is the claim that private initiative should be given a chance.

For 40 years, Keynesian logic has dominated the councils of government. As a philosophy, it has preached that demand can be sustained with government intervention (read: spending). But, in practice, it has encouraged huge corporate profits and complacency through the reduction of competition. It has reduced the will to save and invest because of the corrosive influence of inflation, and it has put people on the public payroll who often do little more than defend their right to be on the public payroll.

Hard issues about municipal services still have to be addressed. But for the first time in a long time, voters are asking the right question: on what are our tax dollars being spent? So far they don't like the answers. And who can blame them?

CHAPTER 1

THE ILLEGITIMATE COLLEGE DEGREE

If events in the late 1960s had a legacy, it was the uprooting of assumptions on which academe depended for 100 years. By suggesting there is no common body of knowledge that should be learned, by rejecting the implicit socializing function of university life and by avoiding competition as a way of engendering excellence, reformers have dramatically changed higher education.

Area distribution requirements have been abandoned at most major universities to be replaced by a free-floating curriculum. Parietals and any other imposed standards of behavior have surrendered to the onslaught of moral relativism. And grades have lost their legitimacy.

Yet even with these changes, the direction of university reforms remains unclear. Few educators have a reasonable idea of what the BA constitutes. At a recent conference someone asked the chairperson, "What is a BA?" He replied, "Oh, it's 120 credits." But the questioner, still understandably dissatisfied, asked, "But what is a credit?" The chairperson unhesitatingly said, "At my college it's $95."

Before 1960, most colleges had a view of the degree that included the accumulation of credit, the satisfaction of a major requirement, the completion

of a project or dissertation and an oral exam or
its equivalent. A degree meant something. The degree
had common coinage.

Surely, there were good reasons for challenging
degree standards. However, the only thing one can
be sure of at the moment is the variation in standards.
At many non-traditional colleges, work, internships,
travel and independent study are equated with courses.
Surely these experiences can be as notable, if not
more notable, than most courses, but how does one
know?

For example, 10 years in the police department
as sergeant qualifies a student for 60 credits. The
assumption is that something had to be learned in
that time and in order to achieve that rank.
Obviously, the assumption is debatable; but even
when the practice is conducted scrupulously, it challenges the meaning of a degree.

Academic credit has meaning because it is linked
to a classroom experience. To give credit for experiences unrelated to a class - regardless of how worthy
- may be appropriate but invariably confusing.

For example, my father worked as a salesman
for 35 years. He was adept at selling anything.
However, whenever I gave him some literature on

advertising, he would say, "I wonder if this author ever tried to sell something to Morris." (Morris was notorious for rejecting any overtures from salesmen). Now if my father applied for academic credit for work experience, how could a fair judgment be made? He obviously knew his job; he was successful at selling, and he would have been the first to admit ignorance of the literature in this field. To grant him credit on the basis of his experience is to suggest that all employees in a similar circumstance are worthy of credit. To reject credit is to apply the standard of the classroom: mastery of a body of literature. But isn't that knowledge supposedly related to performance at some point? And wasn't his performance what business instructors are trying to instill in their students? There are no easy answers.

When 17-year olds announce to parents that they prefer to work rather than attend a university, they are reflecting the spirit of confusion that characterizes the B.A. degree. When employers bark disdainfully at potential employees with college degrees and no skills, they reveal a prejudice about the B.A. degree. And when graduate admissions officers smirk when looking at a transcript, the expression

is usually a response to the ambiguous description
of a degree. These people want a degree with meaning,
indeed, with legitimacy.

Lest this be interpreted as a conventional de-
nunciation of experimental programs for vitiating
degree requirements, that is far from the mark. Universities need experimentation; they also need clear
standards and degrees that have a widely accepted
meaning.

CHAPTER 2
THE POLITICS OF THE CORE CURRICULUM

Like a phoenix rising from the ashes of the late sixties comes a concern for general education, the core curriculum, that now dominates faculty meetings from Cambridge to Berkeley. That this should be happening now is no accident. With the dust almost settled from the period of academic turmoil, it is only natural that faculties consider what damage they have willy-nilly wrought in academe. By adopting egalitarian values, they inevitably vitiated standards. By accepting the student demand for relevance, they abandoned area distribution requirements. And by concentrating their efforts on narrow scholarly areas to the neglect of academic disciplines, faculty members abnegated their authority to administrators and students. In a very real sense, the present concern for general education is not only a desire to re-establish purpose in the curriculum but an attempt by the faculty to reclaim its rightful university role.

This trend, it seems to me, is a healthy antidote to the previous era of vacuous faculty decision making. Recently national education bodies have unequivocally supported faculty plans to design a general education program. The American Council on Education issued a report in which it was noted that "undergraduate degrees should not be awarded...for programs that lack a general/liberal education component." And the Carnegie Council on Policy Studies in Higher Education, while candidly describing general education as a "disaster area," argued that if colleges "cannot deliver an effective general education component, they should seriously consider eliminating it entirely."

Yet while I rejoice at the faculty concern about the curriculum, I remain uneasy about the outcome. What has already emerged is not encouraging. Nowhere can one find a consensual view of appropriate undergraduate experiences. Instead of consensus we see compromise, a compromise that reflects the pluralistic attitudes of most university faculties.

Academics in technical areas of study, for example, who increased the proportion and importance of their courses as general courses lost their legitimacy and glamour have their own narrow interest in general education proposals. They continue to press for a wider array of specialized courses rather than for a holistic approach. But even in the aggregate specialized courses do not add up to a coherent undergraduate program. And the specialists are disinclined to go back to the drawing board to discover their

2

shared assumptions. The result is that in those
institutions that have promoted scholarly specialties
the general education component reflects the specialized orientation of the faculty, whatever that may
be.

Some academics (principally those in the behav-
iorist camp), distressed by the deterioration of basic
skills competence, have entered the general education
debate as minimalists. "If you can train a pigeon
to fly up there and press a button and set off a
bomb," James T. Guines, associate superintendent
of Washington, D.C. schools mused to a WASHINGTON
POST reporter, "why can't you teach human beings
to behave in an effective and rational way?" This
view translates into competency-based instruction,
in which an area of learning is broken down into
its component parts and each part has corresponding
behavioral objectives that are carefully monitored
and measured. There would be few critics of this
approach if, like a simple equation, general education
could be reduced to its component parts. But that
isn't the case. What is worthwhile is very often
not measurable; what is measurable is too often not
very worthwhile. Researchers at the Educational
Research and Development Center took the process

of trivialization to its absurd conclusion by taking
a simple objective - how to handle a book properly -
and breaking it into its measurable components: keeping the book clean, holding it right side up, and
turning the pages correctly.

Behaviorists have promoted a shift from the
educational goals of the classical curriculum, which
were noble but never quite attainable, to goals which
are measurable and attainable but finite. In the
attempt to apply minimum standards of competence
to the general education discussion, they have in-
advertently created a Gresham's Law of curriculum
design: That which is measurable will drive what
is not measurable out of the curriculum.

At a time when many departments are more concerned with survival than principle, the issue of
the core curriculum becomes particularly touchy.
A ballot to determine the complexion of the curriculum is very often simply a pork barrel bid. If
department X can obtain two required courses in the
general education program, it may bolster its sagging
enrollment and thereby save several faculty jobs.
To this end, it will court the good will of others
by voting in favor of department Y's preferred course
selection. Of what value is debate about academic

4

issues in this climate of academic back scratching? Of what use are platitudes when jobs are at stake?

The proliferation of disciplines, subspecialties, and new courses along with ubiquitous fiscal retrenchment in higher education has made it virtually impossible to establish any system of genuine academic priorities. The reigning opinion in academic life is that one discipline is as valuable as another, so long as it leads to personal survival. In some circles it is even argued that one learning experience is as valuable as any other, though admittedly this is still considered a philistine philosophy. But how many contemporary academics would agree with Woodrow Wilson that it is the first duty of the university to bring older wisdom to its constituents: "The world's memory must be kept alive, or we shall never see an end of its old mistakes. We are in danger to lose our identity and become infantile in every generation."

We are well into what Gordon Craig called the age of the "Green Stamp University," in which a student receives as many stamps for T-groups, the Alexander technique, and self-awareness training as for classical philosophy. In such a world, it is difficult to know what a degree means and even more difficult to reconcile competing disciplinary interests so that a coherent curriculum can be established.

There is one further complication. Since educators are now obliged to demonstrate how their degrees assist in securing jobs, the pragmatic dimension of training cannot be ignored in formulating a general education curriculum. It was undoubtedly appropriate for John Stuart Mill to argue that "universities are not intended to teach the knowledge required to fit men for some special mode of making their livelihood." In our own time, however, such neglect seems unconscionable.

The question is how to keep the career component from swamping everything else. Students arrive at the university so career oriented that attempts to discuss life activities other than law or medicine are futile. Since these students vote with their feet, the entire undergraduate curriculum reflects their prejudices. Even more distressing is the unwillingness of parents and legislators to encourage any change in attitude. As one parent put it, "I've lived through noble causes and high ideals; now I just want my kid to live comfortably."

If it was destructive for faculty to bow before every student demand of the last decade, it is equally wrong now to give in to the competing claims of specialists within the academy, of legislators, parents, or any other pressure group. The politics of designing a core curriculum will not disappear, but the effects may be mitigated if faculty remember what they are about. The university exists to train the mind, and that, it seems to me, is the reason for developing a core curriculum. Whether the core curriculum is ultimately effective will depend on the extent to which this vision of a university survives.

CHAPTER 3
TOWARD PLURALISM IN PUBLIC SCHOOLS

Making predictions of any kind is hazardous.
It is an action taken by those who are sufficiently
confident in their guess to accept the consequences
or those who are so capricious they simply don't
care. Since I fall into neither category my prognosis
is based on a variety of scenarios in the hope that
perhaps one will be on target.

My first assumption is that despite a neo-con-
servative trend in the short run, present values
are likely to be extended into the future. This
would include self-indulgence, egotism, hedonism,
materialism and fragmentation. Yet curiously this
very condition allows for a dialectic in educational
systems. If alternatives are sought as a function
of solipsism; if a desire for options is manifested
in new programs, the potential for traditional options
exists as well. Consider, for example, the remarkably
successful parochial school alternative. With little
public support, indeed with liberal disparagement,
these schools do precisely what public schools only
promise. And they do it simply - with order, discipline, rigor and traditional standards.

This is one optimistic alternative. It is also
possible that public school education will price
itself out of existence, both financially and sub-

stantively. We may be unable to afford the cost
and unwilling to sustain the values it espouses.
Teachers' unions may bargain the schools into ever
rising expense for an ever smaller part of the population and engender an increasing community dissatisfaction with the results of their teaching.

Another possibility is a system that stumbles
along relying on modest changes that are introduced
as the latest panacea - the new, new math. Accountability is discussed by educators as the solution
to their problems, but no one knows where the border
is between teacher and parent accountability, much
less teacher and student accountability.

Still another possible scenario is a more pluralistic system than the one we have now. The public
school itself will provide options the way the private
and public sectors do at present. Parents could
decide to send their children to the conventional
program, experimental program "A" or any number of
permutations within the same school.

As I see it, the central educational problem
of the future is the need for choice and the recognition of appropriate educational norms. Without
a recognition of what values the society requires
the schools can do little more than reflect the chaos

and in a subtle way serve to extend it. Choice clearly provides for hope, but it also has the potential to create estrangement and confusion.

How then can an educational system be developed that allows for individual expression and simultaneously avoids fragmentation? This seeming contradiction is not a new problem for the schools. At the turn of the century public school teachers encouraged immigrant children to recognize their independence and at the same time their commitment to the national welfare. Despite the view of the contemporary school revisionists, this effort was quite successful. The schools of the future will require the same effort and result. It seems to me I am not a Pollyanna, by pointing out the resilience of our educational institutions even with the occasional obstinancy of parents, teachers and administrators. It is that resilience that we might rely on to cope with any of the possible educational futures that can be imagined.

CHAPTER 4

SCHOOL SUCCESS: NOT JUST BACK TO BASICS

The litany of criticism aimed at our schools
has become something of a contemporary cliche. Our
students lack discipline. Johnny can't add. Respect
is nonexistent. Scholastic Aptitude Test scores
are declining. And reading is a lost art.

We seem to be spending more money for ever more
dubious ends. And the only matter on which teachers,
administrators and parents are likely to agree is
that something is wrong with the schools.

On what the cause is, there is no consensus.
Parents blame teachers for disappointing student
performance; teachers blame parents for the lack
of student discipline; and administrators direct
blame at everyone but themselves for the problems
they cannot control or even understand. What everyone
ignores is that the school's difficulties are sympto-
matic of societal problems whose remedy or control
is not readily apparent.

At a time when our national values are unclear,
it is no coincidence that our schools don't know
what to teach. When television viewing occupies
the bulk of our time, the role of schools has been
dramatically undermined. With teachers who have
imbibed egalitarian ideology whole hog, it is little
wonder respect for authority is not encouraged. As

technology promises to make "old" approaches to learning obsolete, it seems to make little sense to teach the multiplication table or anything else that requires discipline.

In short, the school is willy-nilly a barometer of national conditions that foster confused goals, a reliance on titillation instead of disciplined study, and an easy route to success.

Curiously enough, the condition of depreciated school performance has occurred just when our expectations of what schools should do are at an all-time high. We now expect the school to be a surrogate parent, to assimilate foreigners, to eradicate social problems other institutions can't handle, to be a church, a moral persuader, and a launching pad for careers.

The failure of other institutions to perform as expected and the gradual loss of legitimacy in many traditional institutions have given the school responsibility in social, economic, political and religious areas. Where the school was once expected to teach the three Rs, it now is expected to do everything under the sun. The consequence is obvious: The school doesn't do what it once did and it can't do what is now expected.

Of course, it wasn't always this way. This view of the schools is a function of the reform ethos that has characterized public education for at least three decades. What we are witnessing in education is the unfolding of a long struggle between two competing ideas of the school.

For a substantial part of our history, and certainly before the mid-19th Century, there were no public schools. But there was unquestionably a public vision of education. Education was considered something of a luxury and the education that was offered stressed a Calvinistic disdain for laziness, a mastery of Greek and Latin and the reinforcement of what was then described as "good citizenship."

Sons did not attend the few private schools and colleges to learn how to become merchants or farmers. That they learned at home in the course of growing up. The college curriculum emphasized five subjects: history, languages, literature, theology and moral philosophy. Presumably, a mastery of this curriculum would enable a young man to be the best he could be and simultaneously serve as guideposts from which to gauge vice, moral deceit, intellectual dishonesty and political sleight-of-hand. One might disagree on who should be educated,

3

but on the matter of what should be studied there was complete accord.

This consensus remained intact until the wave of immigrants eroded a relatively homogeneous society and introduced distinctions between the "true" American and the newcomer who was seen very much as a second-class citizen. Developing parallel to this emerging pluralism was the growth of industry. Factories required cheap raw materials; a large but easily controlled source of cheap labor, and a reservoir of technological skills. Of what possible use were Greek and Latin, history and literature, theology and moral philosophy in this setting?

At the risk of overgeneralization, it could be argued that industrialists, managers and, to some extent, workers eagerly pursuing better jobs, had pragmatic concerns different from the prevailing philosophy of liberal education. By the 1840s, when Horace Mann proposed the public schools, he recognized the need to accommodate the specialization that industry demanded with the traditions of liberal education. As the public schools expanded, pragmatic expertise gradually outpaced the value of a liberal education. In fact, the ideal of a liberal education became ambiguous in an increasingly pluralistic society. This, of course, did not alter the official rhetoric of school officials, but the practice indi- cated that the ability to do, make and predict certain things took precedence over reflection and moral values.

Pragmatism gradually and inexorably - predomi- nated over universal principles in the modern school. What we have witnessed in our own time is simply an extreme version of the same condition. Individual- ism in the open classroom became "doing your own thing." Career preparation became the main focus of one's education. For educators in the school- without-walls experiments, utilitarian goals became the primary educational concern. Contemporary ele- mentary school educators with narrow-gauged goals lost sight of universal liberal arts concerns. And technology created the illusion that everything could be learned without effort.

The evolution of the pragmatic ideal in the schools has created something the businessman could never envision. As sociologist Daniel Bell has indi- cated in another context, capitalism is contradicted by contemporary cultural values, including the values fostered in the schools. Our economic system demands a degree of differentiation; hard work is still required by the economy; some conformity is essential for social control, but educational reforms have served to undermine these values.

Yet, despite the influence of educational reformers, the educational system generally is not organized to change society so much as to reflect changes. It is also not adept at revitalizing itself. But that doesn't preclude developing a synthesis of reform and traditional models to address the school's major problems.

The much discussed educational voucher system, which gives citizens tax money to send their children to the school, public or private, of their choice could be the germ of such a synthesis. The state education department could be empowered to put some reasonable limits on choices, if only to assure educational quality. Obviously, options other than the traditional school will be selected. But if there were fair competition, traditional ideas would at least have a chance of survival. Moreover, the voucher principle is not only applicable to a variety of schools, but to the selection of different programs within a school.

Consider still another reform, schools-without-walls. While the curriculum in this type of education encourages study outside the confines of the school, it is possible to synthesize that idea with specific liberal arts concepts. For example, the economics of scarce resources could be studied in a hospital where the demand for dialysis machines outstrips the supply. Of course as George Bernard Shaw once said, "You can take an ass around the world and it won't become a horse." Some rudimentary principles in economics would have to be learned before the field experience, but the synthesis - if specifically related to a given discipline - could be a great improvement on current practice. The key ingredient is to have curriculum makers who can combine knowledge of a discipline with appropriate field placements.

Similarly, individualized, self-paced instruction might be linked to the study of "great books." Once agreement on the books is reached, a reading schedule can be prescribed in line with the student's reading ability. Since WHAT you read is as important as THAT you read, I am convinced that teachers should recommend appropriate reading matter. Developing an appreciation for good books is as important as achieving a specific reading level.

Like it or not, innovations posing as educational

panaceas will appear and reappear in the schools with predictable frequency. Yet the future of the school is probably more dialectical than present educational critics have considered. Ultimately for any educational notion to succeed it must include universal standards of excellence, an appreciation for ideas not rooted to a specific time and place, the study of books that have stood the test of time, and an acquaintance with moral values.

The test of the future will not be the response to immediate reforms, but the extent to which educators can rediscover traditional standards of excellence and remodel them for the contemporary school. With this in mind, what George Orwell wrote in 1939 has a special poignancy for educators in our time: "We have now sunk to a depth at which the restatement of the obvious is the first duty of intelligent men."

For some time now I've been asking myself why is it that so much potential exists and so little gets done in most universities? Is this inertia related to idiosyncratic conditions in the university or is this simply a bureaucratic fact of life? After thinking about these questions for a while, I have arrived at the conclusion that universities are inert by design; it is a condition of their existence. While I am sure many will balk at this suggestion, my definition of characteristic conditions and actors in a university setting confirms my judgment. Here is one academic's lexicon of university life.

COMMITTEE MEETING - A rite of passage for academics, to determine if their erudition is up to snuff. What is involved, of course, are verbal exchanges to adopt a position that must be reviewed by another committee.

TABLING A MOTION - A polite way of saying we don't like what you're selling but we don't want to offend you by telling you so.

MARKET RESEARCH - One way of determining how to spend university money on something everyone already knows.

CLERK - The one person those in authority will never offend for fear that they will be described as snobs. The reverse is never true; clerks offend everyone regardless of stature or position.

SECRETARY - The person who arrives at 9:30, leaves at 4:00, is always sneezing and takes lunches that would be the envy of Romans. She is also a graduate student who must have some time off to study for exams and more time off to recover from the after-effects.

CHANCELLOR - The person who wishes he were president but is caught in the crosswind of faculty dissatisfaction with the central administration and presidential dissatisfaction with the faculty.

CLASSROOM - A place so bare and unwholesome that one can't help but recall the ecclesiastical origins of the university.

ADMISSIONS - A center for making simple procedures complex through the use of computers and systems analysts.

CURRICULUM - Anything one wants to study.

LIBERAL ARTS - Everything one no longer studies.

CAREER EDUCATION - How to find a job before one graduates so that administrators won't be embarrassed by the number of unemployed alumni.

INDEPENDENT STUDY - A way to allow students with little preparation the opportunity to do what even students with preparation cannot do.

GRADUATION REQUIREMENTS - B.A. - 120 credits; M.A. -

32 to 48 credits; Ph.D - 30 points above the M.A. and a dissertation on such useful topics as "Lighting on A Canton Football Field" or "Volleyball in Tibet" (see Dissertation Abstracts).

A CREDIT - $_____(fill in the amount at your institution).

BOOKSTORE - A place where one buys pens, tee shirts, sweatshirts, records, underwear - almost anything, in fact, except books.

UNIVERSITY LIBRARY - A substitute lounge.

PROFESSIONAL SCHOOL - A place one goes to bank his future.

ORIENTATION - Learning about all the diversions that exist to avoid academic work.

STUDENT EVALUATION - A rite based on the "new" egalitarian view that if students are evaluated they should have the same right. Some simply call it revenge.

SPRING BREAK - University-endorsed Bacchanalia.

DEVELOPMENT OFFICE - Where officials make a silk purse out of a sow's ear.

BUDGET OFFICE - The office that gives you a hundred reasons why your proposal can't be supported.

HONORARY DEGREE - What good works, good connections and public prominence will get you. It doesn't hurt to have a good bank account.

GRADES - Anything between A and C.

INCOMPLETES - A grade used for work that has not been completed. In the days of rigorous standards this was an "F."

STUDENTS - The ones who are given every opportunity to learn, have parents who pay the bills, can enjoy social events almost every night of the week and are always depressed.

REGISTRATION - An insensitive process in which you pay to take courses that you thought you were entitled to take, only to find that the enrollment is closed.

DEPARTMENT CHAIRMAN - The person who shuffles papers instead of teaching courses. His courses are now taught by a graduate assistant who daydreams about shuffling papers instead of teaching courses.

FACULTY - Those who teach students, do research, attend committee meetings, involve themselves in community affairs and are told by administrators that they are unproductive.

PURCHASING OFFICE - Its slogan: "Anything we can buy you can buy cheaper."

GRADUATE STUDY - The courses are no more difficult than those taken by undergraduates; the professors no more sophisticated and the workload no more trying. Why then "graduate study?" It helps the cash register

4

ring by charging more for its credit.

LATIN HONORS - An undifferentiated honor conferred on all those with 3.0 g.p.a. or better; in other words 95 per cent of the graduating class.

RESIDENCY REQUIREMENTS - A sufficient number of credits to be eligible for a degree from a given program. What is sufficient? Ask any advisor.

MAJOR - Presumably an area of study where one gains expertise. In fact it is a study in the use of jargon. Did you ever hear a psychology major refer to "conscience" instead of "superego"?

MINORS - An area of study where one learns only some jargon, enough to distinguish him from a major.

DORMITORIES - Places that encourage certain practices every night of the week that swinging singles reserve for the weekends.

REGISTRAR - A person who maintains records so diligently that they can never be released for fear that a smudge might change a B+ to a B-.

SYLLABUS - What a professor's course is all about before student objections.

PREREQUISITES - What courses you are supposed to have had in order to gain entry into an advanced course, unless you simply ask for permission to take it.

5

TENURE - What colleagues do for one another. In the case of rejection, it is what colleagues do to one another.

COMMENCEMENT - When the student with the highest grades says what the faculty wants to hear, even though they don't listen.

BOARD OF TRUSTEES - The people with money and clout who are trying to find out why the university is in debt.

AREA DISTRIBUTION REQUIREMENTS - An anachronism based on the supposition that a college student should have courses in various disciplines. Its demise began when the principle was eroded by political and economic concerns. "We'll trade one history course for one dance therapy course."

INTERDISCIPLINARY PROGRAM - The cultivated ignorance of any one discipline.

EXPERIMENTAL PROGRAMS - Innovative, non-traditional offerings seeking new constituencies. Since there are no "new constituencies," these programs are any that one chooses to call "experimental."

PROMOTION - What happens if you've been loyal, diligent and published in the magazine section of the NEW YORK TIMES.

ADVISEMENT - Signing student programs.

6

COUNSELING - Asking what a student's career plans are before signing his program.

GRADUATE TEACHING FELLOW - The "migrant worker" at the university who is exploited with little salary and heavy teaching loads. His reward is a letter of recommendation for a nonexistent position.

INTERCOLLEGIATE SPORTS - Big business on the campus or how to make money without classrooms and instructors.

LIFE EXPERIENCE - A ploy for giving adult students advanced standing for being married, maintaining a job, having children, living in the ghetto, reading books and having a pulse rate over one.